P9-CKX-509

A WOMAN
MAKES
A PLAN

life

A WOMAN
MAKES
A PLAN

Advice for a Lifetime of
Adventure, Beauty, and Success

———— ◆ ————

MAYE MUSK

VIKING LIFE

VIKING
An imprint of Penguin Random House LLC
penguinrandomhouse.com

A Viking Life Book

Library of Congress Cataloging-In-Publication Control Number: 2019039058

ISBN 9781984878502 (hardcover)
ISBN 9781984878519 (ebook)

Printed in the United States of America
1   3   5   7   9   10   8   6   4   2

BOOK DESIGN BY LUCIA BERNARD

I would like to dedicate this book to the people
who have influenced my life the most:

My late mother, Wyn Haldeman, who gave me, my sisters,
and every woman she met the confidence to do well.

My late sister, Lynne Haldeman, who listened to my struggles
every night for five years and encouraged me through my
co-op court case to repair my building's chimney.

My twin sister, Kaye, who has protected me all my life,
and who keeps me down-to-earth.

Tosca, my lovely daughter, and Elon and Kimbal, my two
sons, who have respected and supported me in everything I do.

My eleven grandchildren, who keep me learning
and bring me so much joy with all their questions.

My extended family, friends, and team, who have
supported me throughout my hard, good, and new times.

CONTENTS

Part 5: Health

CONCLUSION

LIVE DANGEROUSLY—CAREFULLY

Make a plan, and take a chance

I grew up in a family that had an airplane and a fascination for exploration. My parents flew across Canada, America, Africa, Europe, Asia, and Australia in a small, canvas-covered propeller plane with no GPS or radio. When we were children, they took us on trips to the Kalahari Desert every winter to search for the lost city. Looking back, I realize it was dangerous to go across the desert with a compass and three weeks' supply of water and food with five kids. But my father and mother planned our trips to the last detail. Our family motto was "live dangerously—carefully." My father sought adventure, but he knew to be ready for the unexpected. Because of that, I'm always curious and willing to explore. And I know that I can take a risk as long as I'm prepared.

There is an Afrikaans saying that I grew up with: *"'N boer maak 'n plan."* It literally translates to "a farmer makes a plan," and it's something people said all the time in South Africa. It could be small, or it could be huge, but we used it any time we needed to change direction and fix a problem. Whatever obstacle is in front of you, you have to address it and find another way to sort it out.

At first I wanted this book to be called *Struggling and Surviving,* but that didn't sound very compelling to anyone. I hope when you read this book that you will struggle less and survive more than I did. In my life, things have gone wrong way too often, and each time I have had to make a plan. You can plan things as a woman, but then you get sideswiped, and you have to make another plan. (By the way, this happens to men, too.)

I have started my life over many times, and as an adult I've lived in nine cities across three countries. I don't recommend starting over again and again like I did, but if you have to, you must plan ahead. You can live a more exciting and happier life if you take chances. I took a lot of chances and struggled in the beginning, but I persisted until I found success in my personal and business lives. You don't have to plan every detail of the changes in your life; you can sort out your problems as they come along. And there will be different problems, of course. But you just have to plan that first step.

There are surprises around every corner in life. From taking care of yourself and your family and friends, to looking and feeling fantastic, to having a successful career and living an adventurous life—it's a lot to think about all at once. But if you start with your first step, and then the next step after that, you can keep on moving ahead.

When I was in bad situations, I read many romance or self-help books. They gave me hope. Perhaps sharing my experiences with you will give you hope, too.

Being my age is fantastic. I have lived for seven decades, enjoyed two successful careers, and raised three children. I'm a grandmother to eleven. And now, I'm more in demand than ever as a wellness speaker and model. I was even asked to write this book! That's why I say that it's great to be seventy-one! I wake up excited for each day.

If you have a good attitude and you make a plan and take a chance, even Mars is possible.

PART ONE

———— ♦ ————

Beauty

ONE

SILVER IS THE NEW BLOND

Life keeps getting better

◆

At fifty-nine years old, I let my hair go silver. Two years later, I was pregnant on the cover of *New York* magazine. (Well, I wasn't really pregnant, but it looked pretty convincing.) At sixty-seven, I walked in my first runway show at New York Fashion Week with women who were a third of my age. At sixty-nine, I became a CoverGirl.

Can you imagine? I never did. I would never have predicted that letting my hair go gray would be the secret to becoming a supermodel. I first walked a runway at fifteen, and they told me I'd be done at eighteen. As a model, I never expected to be carrying on this long—and certainly not in my prime at seventy-one. But here I am, fifty-six years later, and I'm still just getting started.

Women don't have to slow down as they age. I'm running like

a speeding bullet. Exploring everything, having fun, working more than ever, working on social media to make sure that I'm working more than ever, and having the most fun. Did I mention fun? If men don't have to slow down, we shouldn't have to either. Don't let aging slow you down or stop you from moving ahead. Look after yourself as best you can by eating well, smiling, and being active, happy, and confident. I have never been afraid of aging. Funny enough, when I see the wrinkles on my face—and after sixty, wrinkles on my thighs and my arms—I find them amusing. I'm just so happy to be in good health.

I started modeling as a teenager in Pretoria, South Africa, because a friend of my parents' ran a modeling school and agency. Her name was Lettie, and her husband had a plane, like my father. Every Sunday night, they would have dinner with our family. Lettie was very beautiful and graceful, and she had a quiet confidence that made you want to do what she asked you to.

When my twin sister, Kaye, and I were fifteen, Lettie invited us to do her modeling course for free, which we did without giving it much thought. For the final walk, the one that would get us our diplomas, I made myself a pink suit in the style of Chanel. I had my brown hair done, and I did my own makeup.

Lettie was the one who started hiring me to model, too. I would do runway shows on Saturday mornings in a department store when she asked, or print jobs. I didn't feel special or privileged about being a model. It was just a job. It was better-paying than other jobs, which was nice, but when I found that out, it surprised me. You went somewhere, you put on a dress, you walked around the room, you went home. Why would that be well-paid? But it was, especially for a girl my age.

I had no idea back then that I would still be a model at seventy-one. You just had to look around the room at these things to understand that all the models were very young. I knew it was temporary, and it didn't bother me at all. I was just happy to get paid. My goal wasn't to model; it was to go to university.

I still modeled in university, to my surprise. As planned, I got my degree, and then I got married: another surprise. My goal wasn't to have children so quickly either. I didn't realize I could fall pregnant on a honeymoon and have three kids in three years. Elon, Kimbal, and Tosca were three more surprises. With each child, I added a few blond highlights to my hair. After Tosca, I was completely blond.

I started modeling again after I'd had my three kids, because Lettie asked me to. Her agency needed somebody to do mother-of-the-bride runway shows, and they couldn't have an eighteen-year-old do it. All the other girls were too young. So she asked me, because I was a very grown-up twenty-eight. In this way, I became the oldest model in South Africa.

I moved to Durban as a single mother at thirty-one because I was running away from my husband. I couldn't afford to have anybody else color my hair anymore, so I started doing it myself and it became various shades of blond and orange. Blorange, as they call it. It was pretty bad. Very frizzy, and I was cutting it myself to save money. They still let me model for some reason, so I didn't worry about it. It didn't affect my nutrition practice, which I had started at twenty-two in my apartment in Pretoria, in any case. As long as I could help my clients, they didn't pay attention to what my hair looked like.

At forty-two, when I moved to Toronto, I went to school for my PhD while I modeled and taught, keeping current in both professions. I had a model portfolio that showed that I could get work, so a Toronto agency was willing to take me on because they thought they could make money with me. Most of the modeling jobs out there were for younger women, but sometimes they just needed an older model in order to make it look realistic. That was when I did my first grandmother ad, a front cover. I was only forty-two!

I was not the only model in Toronto in my forties, of course. While usually I'd be the only person at a modeling job who wasn't in my teens or twenties, that was not always the case. Remember, this was not high fashion or haute couture. This was not New York Fashion Week or Milan.

I remember once doing a runway show where it was all older women and guys. Afterward, we all went out for a drink. One of the guys said to me, "You're going to have to buy your own drink, because you're the only person who hasn't been in bed with me."

I just looked at him.

He said, "Yeah, I've done mattress ads with all the other models."

That was the kind of job available for older models. Advertisements for sales on beds, and that kind of thing.

I didn't care, because I wasn't there to be exciting. It was just work, and I needed to work. I kept modeling because it was fun, kept me looking good, and got me away from the office to explore different cities and to meet new people. In those years, they had to book me three weeks ahead of time to not disrupt my practice, and I wouldn't model more than four days a month. It paid as much as my dietetics practice, which was my stable and basic income, and I wasn't going to rock that boat—that would cover everyday expenses, rent, bus fare, school uniforms, gas, and car services. Modeling enabled me to buy a cheap flight to visit family, some clothes, or something we needed for the apartment. Sometimes I would get a dress. Modeling was the cherry on top.

I didn't even tell my nutrition clients I modeled, and because there was no social media, nobody knew.

Sometimes someone would say, "Is that you in a magazine?"

And I'd say, "Yes. I'm the Sears housecoat queen."

That was my job. If Sears had a housecoat, they called me in to make it look good.

By the time I was in my fifties, I was living in New York. I did a few great campaigns, then signed with a bigger agency, because I thought it would increase my exposure. It did the opposite. I went from sometimes modeling to barely modeling.

I'd email and say I didn't join them to stop modeling. They would write back to say that there was no work for me.

I'd call. They'd say, "They just don't want to see you. They prefer the other models who are better-known than you."

I would think, "But they're not that well-known either."

I couldn't understand why the clients never wanted to see

me anymore. I'd been modeling for decades, but maybe it was time. I was told that nobody liked my look anymore.

By chance, I would run into some people who worked in the business. They would stop me in the street or in a restaurant and say, "We've been trying to book you, but you're never available."

I would go to the agency and say, "People have been trying to book me."

"No, they haven't. They're getting you mixed up with somebody else."

That was when I decided on my own to stop coloring my hair. I thought, "Well, I'm barely modeling. I might as well see what color I am underneath."

My hair started to grow out, and it looked terrible. There was a white patch on top and blond hair at my shoulders. As a dietitian, it doesn't matter what color hair you have, as long as you're good. On the advice of my best friend, Julia Perry, I cut my hair very short. It was an edgy, exciting look, nothing like I'd ever done before.

After I went gray, the agency didn't send me out for six months. It was a very painful period. It started to seem as though there would be no more opportunities for me there, that perhaps this was the end of my modeling career.

Then something interesting happened. A casting director called my agency to book me for the cover of *Time* magazine. This time my agency couldn't say that I was not available, as the director's office was a block away from my home and she saw me walking my dog every morning.

Then they had to book me for the job. That was how I wound up in *Time* magazine, on the front page of the Health section.

I realized that there *was* work out there for me. It wasn't about my look. It was about my agency.

I needed a plan.

Everybody has their own agenda. I wanted to take advantage of whatever work opportunities existed for me. My agents should have been promoting my career, but for some reason, they weren't. Once I understood this, I had to deal with it. I couldn't just stand by and let someone else keep work from me.

I went down to the agency to speak my mind, because if you want something, you have to ask for it.

My agent was irate.

"How dare you think we're not working hard for you!"

She was lying. We both knew it. It's one thing to go to an audition and not get the job. That had happened to me many, many times. You go and you wait in line and so do twenty other women, and you don't get the job. That is part of being a model. Not being sent to castings by your representation— that's bad.

They refused to admit it. They kept insisting that there was no work. I was stuck, because I had a contract.

When you're in a bad work situation that isn't changing and you want to get out of it, you can't be sure about what will happen next. It is scary. You will have a miserable time at work every day. If you are not experiencing any joy, your day will be gloomy.

You need to look forward to your work and love it, because you spend most of your waking hours working. In my dietetics practice, I had many female lawyer clients who loved their work but didn't like their bosses. I know that because their unhappiness and stress made them eat poorly. I would tell them to change their situation. They would make a change, go to a new law firm or start off on their own, and they would be happier and eat better. My clients always said I was cheaper than a psychologist.

I looked at my model contract, and I saw that it covered New York City only. So I contacted agents in Philadelphia. The Hamptons. Connecticut. New Jersey. LA, Hamburg, Munich, Paris, London. I signed with those agencies, and I started getting some work. I began to go to Europe to shoot catalogs, to do some editorial work, or for hair and pharmaceutical ads. It paid well, for me, and I always flew economy and traveled on a budget.

Closer to home, I was doing catalogs, commercials, and showroom work. It wasn't glamorous, but it was work. The job was to show clothes to clients of inexpensive department stores. I would have a little tiny cardboard cubicle to change in, and then I'd come out. There would be thirty people sitting there, watching me wear the clothes. In between outfits I'd go back to that little cubicle, where I had a bagel with cream cheese, and every time I got changed, I would just take a small bite, because I didn't have time to eat a whole bagel.

Most of the jobs were in New York, and I was still being held back from those opportunities. I knew that I could do better. I knew that it was not my age or my looks standing in my way. It was them, not me!

I had to find a way around it. I went and sat in their waiting room, and I sat there, and I sat there, and I sat until they sent me in to see the senior person.

I said to her, "I haven't had a casting for six months. You've got to let me go."

I was determined not to leave until I had gotten what I wanted, and eventually they agreed. I should've done that sooner. Please learn quicker than I did, and you will suffer less. If it's not going to change, get out of it as soon as you can, even if you end up having nothing afterward or thinking you'll have nothing afterward. Or be financially strapped afterward.

That was when I joined a boutique agency that had worked with me before. They were excited to work with me, and they loved my new look. They sent me to do an editorial in Toronto, which was remarkable, because as you got older, nobody wanted you for editorials. Editorial work was cool. I wasn't cool. I had no idea how to pose for an editorial!

For catalogs, you're relaxed, and you're a happy person, and you don't crease the garment. You don't pull it in a funny angle. In an editorial, suddenly there's license to leap and dance and stretch out and do crazy stuff. I had to learn, so I started looking in magazines.

The only editorial experience I had was when I was forty-five, and in that shoot I was the awkward background for the supermodel they were featuring.

I flew to Toronto. I was the only model at the shoot.

I said, "Where are all the other models?"

They said, "No, you're the only one."

Then I was in this creative world of designer, couture, beautiful clothes. They shot a white story, eight pages in white outfits. It was so beautiful. A different hairstyle every time, even with the short hair.

When I saw it, all I could say was, "Wow."

Then the bookings started coming in. When I had first moved to New York, Kimbal and I were in Times Square, looking up at all the giant ads, and I told him, "One day I'll be in one of those." We both chuckled. And now there I was: on a fifteen-foot-tall billboard in Times Square for the first time.

I had gone to a casting with three hundred women for a Virgin America advertisement, and they booked me. At the shoot, there was a young girl and a young man there as well, very young models, too fabulous to talk to me. Yet on the final billboards, I was the face you saw. At sixty-seven, I was everywhere: in Times Square, on the subways, and in every airport in America. You couldn't get off a train or on a plane without seeing my face.

Who knew things would take off when I went silver?! At fifteen, I had been told I'd be done by eighteen, and at seventy-one, I'm the biggest I've ever been. What I've learned is that you can always find a way. You can always make another plan. Of course, it took time for me to learn, and I'm still learning!

Something else happened that was a huge surprise. Social media! Through my postings, people would absolutely love my white hair, and modeling jobs would be booked because of the color of my hair. Now I'm very happy to walk into a room knowing I'm the only person in it with white hair. If there is another woman with white hair, I always smile and say, "Matchy-matchy."

One thing I am sure of is that it just gets better. Every Monday, I'm more excited than ever, because I'm expecting some fun work to happen. Even if nothing happens, I'm still excited to post on my social media and website to make that happen. That's why I say that it's great to be seventy-one. That's why I don't worry about age.

I'm too busy having fun.

TWO

BE FASCINATING

It's better to be interesting than to be beautiful

◆

I was in my fifties when I went to a casting for a beauty ad. The casting director said, "Oh, you're so beautiful."

I said, "Well, isn't that the prerequisite?"

I mean, I was coming for a beauty campaign. I thought I was hilarious, because having grown up in South Africa, I was accustomed to people being very self-deprecating.

They were horrified. They didn't find me funny at all . . . I wasn't even considered for that job, because I was too cheeky.

After that, I learned to just say, "Thank you."

I have never understood why everybody in America talks about being beautiful. In South Africa, you are more valued as a woman if you're intelligent and interesting and have a good sense of humor. Rather than your outer look. People said, "You're funny." And I thought I was. And I think I am. They were more interested in my work as a dietitian, and that I was up to date on research and giving talks. And doing media work. And had my practice. They were more interested in my work ethic and professionalism.

When I first got to America, I called my twin sister, Kaye, to tell her about this American quirk of talking about being beautiful.

My sister Kaye is one of my favorite people. We talk every night, and she tells me the truth about everything. She is the person I go to for advice about everything from investments to whether I should get veneers (she said no). She's always been there for me and always been supportive of me.

The best thing about Kaye is that she's straight-talking and takes no nonsense at all. She just says what she thinks.

That doesn't mean that she is a serious person. Kaye is always laughing, and between us, she is the fun one. Except she isn't trying to amuse anybody except herself. The result is that people love her to bits, and everybody hovers about her when she begins speaking. If you met her, you'd love her, too. Once someone has met Kaye, I might as well sit in the corner knitting. Unfortunately, you will never meet her, as she's a hermit.

Kaye said, "People always thought you were beautiful, even if they didn't say it. When you walked into a room, people always looked at you."

I haven't even noticed, because I wasn't looking at anybody. I was just looking where I was going. It made me remember guys I dated over the years who would say, "Maye, when we walk into the restaurant, will you walk in front of me?"

I would, and then they would join me so that everyone could see they were with me. Of course, they'd wind up dumping me anyhow, because that's what people who can only see the outside will do.

I should have dropped them first. When you meet someone who is beautiful, of course you would like to enjoy their company. If they are not interesting, you will move away very quickly. It's better to have people like you for your personality rather than for your outside beauty.

I remember meeting a couple; he was so handsome and she was plain. It seemed like an odd couple. Until the moment she started talking—then she was the most magnetic person in the room.

It was her attitude. It was her confidence. It was the way she looked at life. She became a good friend, because she was so intelligent and so much fun. I couldn't get enough of her.

There are very many things a person can be. I'd rather my gravestone read "She was funny" than "She was beautiful."

Being obsessed with outer beauty can create insecurities if you aren't perfect-looking. It could make you unhappy and stop you from developing many other characteristics that are wonderful, like intelligence or being fun and interesting.

My advice is to be kind to others, listen to others, and be upbeat. Don't start talking about your miserable life. Show confidence, respect, interest in others, and smile; that will make you fascinating. Everyone has a talent that they can share with other people. If at the moment you feel as though you don't have any talents, go to a time in the past when you felt confident about some aspect of your life. Work on that section, study it, share it, and become more interesting. If you have a profession, a hobby, or a special interest, read about it, and mention it in conversations. Be excited about it, and you'll be more interesting and more intelligent. You don't have to be good at everything, but you need to be good at something. When people ask me about recipes, I cannot help them because I'm not a good cook. I don't feel bad about it; it's just not my talent nor interest. I am certainly not going to experiment with new foods to impress everyone, when I don't enjoy it. Be sure to be good at something you enjoy.

Also, try to have a sense of humor, and be less sensitive about what people are saying. When a man wants to date me, and I say no, he will say he can find someone younger than me. I just laugh. I don't care what he can find; I am not interested in him, and I'm certainly not going to be upset about it.

We need to move on and be happy with ourselves. If you can speak with a sense of humor, laugh at yourself, and add lightness in your voice, you will be more fun. It's hard not to talk about yourself, especially if you're going through a hard time, but you need to be fascinating.

THREE

GREAT MODEL, DRESSES TERRIBLY

You don't have to be stylish; just find a stylish friend

◆

I used to dress glam once or twice a year for my birthday or a wedding. Only when I was sixty-seven and went to the Met Ball, a huge fashion gala, as Elon's guest, did I know how much preparation goes into walking the red carpet. When I'm in a glam dress, I feel fantastic. I walk taller, stand up straighter, smile at everyone, and have an extra bounce in my step.

Now I appreciate how much a glam team does to prepare celebrities for the red carpet of awards shows and film premieres. Designers, stylists, and stylist assistants all stress out finding the perfect outfit. What you don't realize is that the perfect undergarment makes the dress fall nicely. Also, accessories are important, from demure to dramatic. Hair needs to look different every time so people know that you're making an extra effort. Makeup people will decide on the "no makeup" natural look (still takes an hour) or high-glamour look with false lashes and major contour. Now I know it takes a village. You should appreciate this in celebrities, too.

When I go to an event dressed wonderfully, it's because Julia Perry, who has been my best friend and stylist for nearly thirty years, is dressing me.

I met Julia when I was forty-three years old. I had finished my second master's degree in Toronto, and I was struggling to build my nutrition practice. My modeling career proved useful, because an agency that ran a modeling school offered me free use of an office if I would model for them and teach at their modeling school in the evenings. I was teaching runway, print, and professionalism, and for the first time, I had my own office, away from home. It was very exciting, and I felt like a professional.

It took only a month before they asked if I would be the director of the modeling school, because the woman who ran the program was disorganized. I was known to be very reliable and punctual, which is a huge advantage. I offered to teach wardrobe, too—I used to teach wardrobe in South Africa, but I had no idea how little I really knew about it.

They brought in an expert, and as soon as she began to talk, I realized that I knew nothing about wardrobe. She began to speak about the four seasons and the different colors and different textures . . . I was blown away.

And that was how I met Julia. For her part, she will tell you that she was having her own reaction to me.

"Here was this beautiful woman," she will say, "who is

teaching this modeling school. Great model, dresses terribly. Just terribly."

Even though I am always dressed in the latest fashions these days, that's not how it was for most of my life. When I was a child, my mother made all her own clothes, and she made ours, too. As a teenager, I learned to sew so that I could make clothes for myself. I made bell-bottoms and tent dresses. I could even make a suit. At first, I followed a pattern, and then my mom sent me to pattern-cutting classes so that I could make clothes that were in magazines but not yet available in patterns. If I wanted to wear high fashion, I had to make it myself.

As a professional, when I was choosing my clothes for work, I would mainly wear suits. I did not wear anything that was clingy or tight, because I was counseling. I would wear a suit and walk into a room with confidence because I felt good about it. I thought that it looked smart and that I looked trust-worthy.

My daughter, Tosca, would say, "Are you going to wear a gray suit again, or will you wear a navy blue suit again?"

Because what I wore never varied.

I always cared about myself. I just didn't have such good taste. Fortunately, I didn't realize that. Why would I? I was surrounded by scientists, and we were really focused on research work and doing good things for other people, how to keep them in good health. We just loved our work. I was more stylish than my scientist friends, so of course all my colleagues thought I dressed fabulously. And I felt very confident.

Then I met Julia. Julia told me that I should be dressing better. She insisted that instead of having a lot of those suits, I should have only one suit that fit better and was a better-quality material, and she said that she could help me with my wardrobe. I needed her help, but I could not afford to pay her, so we agreed that I would give her a nutrition consultation in exchange for a style consult. I think that I improved her eating habits, and she says that I did, and that I still do. I know that the advice she gave me changed my life.

Before Julia, I didn't fully understand how to put myself together for maximum impact. After Julia, I looked as confident on the outside as I felt on the inside, and I am convinced that the success I have found in both of my careers is related to the advice she gave me about how I dressed.

Julia came and looked through my clothes, to start, and threw out nearly everything. I was left with just a few things to wear.

"Now," said Julia, "you have to buy a suit, two blouses, one pair of shoes, and a bag. All right?"

I said, "I can't afford to buy anything."

She said, "You've got to look as good as your clients." I was still struggling with money, so I agreed that we could do it in stages. I didn't need very much. Since my clients saw me once a week, I didn't need something different for every day.

The first time I wore that outfit, one that was cut right, that was made of a beautiful fabric, well, I did feel more confident.

As I earned money, Julia wanted me to continue to build my wardrobe, but I didn't have any time to spare. I was working too much to spend my time shopping.

She said, "Block out an hour."

The department stores were nearby, so she would go there,

put out all the things she thought were important, like the second suit, the shoes and blouses, casual wear, a coat. I would dash over during my break, try everything on quickly, and pay for whatever I chose before I had to get back to my office. We would fit once every two months. That was how she built up my wardrobe.

If you wish to be stylish but find it complicated, like I do, find a friend who has great style. Usually they love to go shopping. Ask her or him to take you shopping to choose some of your basic items, as well as something fabulous for a special occasion. They also should choose your accessories, like earrings, necklaces, handbags, shoes, hose. You need the complete look. When they do make their choices, you are going to feel very uncomfortable and strange in these outfits. I do, all the time, but I've received so many compliments that I have to trust someone else who has more style than me. Be willing to change, make mistakes, change again, until you get the right style for you.

Most of my life I was not wealthy and still managed to dress as stylish as my limited talent could achieve. You could make clothes like I did for many years. Buying a pattern and inexpensive material can make you a pretty dress. Of course, you have to have a sewing machine, too. There are inexpensive clothing stores and discount clothing outlets. I would sometimes take a friend there to help me buy clothes. When I was new in Toronto, a friend took me to a discount store and made me buy a $10 miniskirt at forty-two. I was so embarrassed, but everyone loved it. People always think you need a lot of money to look good. But speaking as someone who struggled financially for many years, you need to look at it as part of your overall yearly spending. Similar to budgeting for haircuts or dentist visits. If you have only $500 to spend twice a year, there are great sales, thrift shops, and rental places that can help you with two to three outfits that complements your lifestyle and work. The investment is worth it. You just need a plan.

Here is mine: twice a year, my friend Julia comes to my apartment to go through my wardrobe. We are constantly streamlining down to the best and the basics. To do this, take everything out of your closet and drawers. Put back clothes and accessories that fit you and you enjoy wearing. Repair those that need repairing.

Streamlining my wardrobe down to the pieces I really will wear makes getting dressed a pleasure instead of a chore. There are plenty of people who read fashion blogs and spend hours shopping or trying on different outfits. They just love it. That isn't me! I do enjoy dressing nicely, but I don't want to spend a lot of time on it every day. That's why we are often going through what I have, pulling out the clothes I haven't been wearing, and putting them in donation bags for Dress for Success. These clothes are perfectly good and clean; they don't suit me anymore, but they will make someone else very happy. I wish they'd been around in Toronto when I couldn't afford a coat.

If you're not constantly grooming your wardrobe, it's likely that half the things hanging in your closet are too small, too large, need repairs, or just no longer feel like you. The main thing is that the clothes have to fit. Because as soon as they're too big, you look frumpy. When they're too tight, you look terrible.

Julia and I agree that a nice foundation of basics is a good base; then you can add a gold hoop or a nice pair of jeans and a cool boot. Start with the simple things: Your day-to-day stuff, like black jeans that look sexy with anything. Fake leather leggings that you can wear with a sweater or a button-down shirt. A great gray wool coat or trench coat. Great T-shirts and those earrings that you can wear with anything. If you're just starting to build your wardrobe or you need a sharp update, invest in a great blazer or jacket. This will add to your existing pieces and add to your presence.

Then, once you have the basics, it becomes so much fun to add color. A green or pink cardigan or something that you throw over everything, or a funky belt that you can use to change the look of your trench coat. High-quality leather goods are another way to add mileage to existing clothing pieces and add polish to your image. When Julia started working with my wardrobe, she got rid of my handbag collection and replaced it with one good leather bag. Even when I was on a budget, she taught me that quantity is not important and that quality is, so I learned to spoil myself with one good item and not feel guilty. This way we can be sustainable and fashionable at the same time, wearing things over and over and not buying many new items.

The moral of the story is: You don't have to be stylish to dress well. You just need a stylish friend.

I'll see other women, sometimes, who have white hair like mine. They'll say, "I love your dress."

I'll say, "Well, you can wear it, too!"

They say, "I couldn't."

Many women think they can't. Women my age, women of all ages, won't try. I know because I used to be like that.

Julia would say, "Wear this!"

I'd say, "No, I won't!"

I'd try to resist, but she wouldn't budge. At every one of my big birthday parties, she would ignore me when I said a dress was too tight or too glamorous. I'm so glad that she did, because the photos ended up looking wonderful!

That's why now I say yes, because I've learned that if I try it, I will probably love it. If I don't, so what? It's just clothes. You can try looks that terrify you, because you also don't have to wear it again. None of it is permanent.

I wasn't bold in the past but now I am. Being part of many fashion editorials and test shoots where themes are so creative, I'm often styled in bold or unexpected ways. Now I'm more fashion curious and even adventurous, putting my looks in the hands of my high-fashion team. Many times I look at myself in the mirror before heading out for an event wondering, "What is my stylist thinking? I just don't get this look." But I enjoy

the reactions I receive from photographers, friends, and strangers at not looking like a typical seventy-plus-year-old and having fun with fashion. What took me so long?

Once you receive a compliment, you will feel great, walk taller, smile more, and get comfortable with your new fashion style. Give it a try.

FOUR

I LOVE MAKEUP, AND MAKEUP LOVES ME

Makeup can change your look and mood

◆

Being a fascinating person doesn't mean you have to look drab on the outside. I love makeup because it takes my plain face, a blank canvas, and paints it into a work of art. I have sunspots on my face and dark rings under the eyes, and, yes, wrinkles. A good foundation and concealer smooth out the color of my skin. I have very few eyebrows and eyelashes, as well as thin lips. An eyebrow pencil shapes my face nicely. Eye makeup opens up my eyes and makes them look larger. Mascara even more so. False eyelashes make me look glamorous and red carpet ready. Lip liner on the outside of my lips makes my lips larger, and gloss plumps up the lips. Makeup reduces my wrinkles, makes my eyes larger, and contours my cheeks. And that's why I wear it.

Every look can be different, with different colors of eyeshadows and lipsticks. Experimenting is fun. It feels amazing to see the results when I'm done.

I've been wearing makeup since I was a young teenager. It was the sixties, and I studied Twiggy in magazines. Copying her look took a lot of work, with a black line in the crease of our eyes, false eyelashes on top and the single false eyelashes on the bottom; we would also paint lower eyelashes. It would take an hour, and it was fun. We loved that because it made us look fabulous and fashionable. My dad would come along and say, "It's too much."

The problem is, with fashion, we have to change. So when natural makeup came into fashion, I had to change my makeup routine completely. In the sixties, along with Twiggy makeup, we wanted very thin eyebrows. I did such good plucking work with the tweezers that mine never grew back. I don't think I had many to begin with! But I tweezed out what I had.

As soon as the style changed, I had to learn how to fill them in.

I still fill them in! That's the joy of makeup. I'm not good at doing my eyebrows, but at least that way I have them!

Now I am seventy-one, and I still get to play dress-up for the red carpet or to walk a runway. But that's not how I dress every day! Most of the time, when I'm at home, there's no makeup, just clean skin and lip balm. I don't wear makeup when I'm running errands with my dog, or on my computer during the day, or picking up my grandchildren from school. I put on makeup when I'm going out to lunch, or to meet friends, or to a meeting.

My makeup routine always starts with a clean and moisturized face. My skin care routine is simple. I use a face wash at home and soap and water when traveling. I put on eye cream and then moisturizer with at least SPF 15 for a sunny day. In the evening, I cleanse my face to take off any makeup I may have been wearing that day, and then I put on an eye cream and night cream.

Always wear sunscreen! If you skip makeup, that's up to you. If you're skipping sun precautions, you're asking for trouble. I can't tell you how many women worry about skin care and then lie in the sun for what I call "skin uncare." The best decision a person can make is to protect their skin in the sun, like wearing a hat and using sunscreen.

I do my own makeup unless there is a red carpet. If I do my makeup for a red carpet, I look washed-out. When it's professionally done, it is highlighted and more glamorous. Sometimes there's a green eyeshadow, sometimes gold in the corners. Really different for a woman in her seventies. The social media comments are positive, so we just keep trying. Comments like "fierce"; "on fire"; "GOAT," which means "Greatest of All Time"; and "OG," for "Original Gangster." Now that's really funny.

I take ten minutes when I do my own makeup. Makeup artists take one hour. Even if I took an hour, I wouldn't be able to create the right look because I don't have that talent. Those people are artists! I'm a scientist, and I don't have the talent to do what the artists do. But even people who aren't artists can do some good work with makeup if they have a few simple tools and they learn how to use them. I know one makeup artist who has a suitcase for all her colors and tools. Fifty-two pounds of tools and makeup, and she brings it with her on flights. And she always has to pay the fee for extra weight, but she needs those two extra pounds of tools. Because that's her job.

I'm lucky to have my friend Julia as an artistic director when I dress up for an event. And we get to decide together who I'm going to be for the evening. She is thinking about what she can do to ensure that I'm going to stand out.

How will they do my hair? How will they do my makeup? Will I look fresh? Are we going to do a dramatic eye shadow? A strong lipstick? She may ask for gold, for purple, for blue. She's also thinking about where we are going, because the character that is being created is for a specific event. Is it a film event? Is it a book launch? Is it a charity event? Then they get to work. It's like a costume party.

When I was chosen as a CoverGirl at sixty-nine, it was a huge and fantastic surprise. I had done makeup campaigns before, but not one with me as the main model. I was very excited. Now America could see that makeup was good for all ages. I have never been asked to look younger, nor felt the need to hide my age. I'm so happy to be seventy-one! I am so happy to let people know that this is how fabulous we can look. As women, makeup can improve our look. Let's take advantage of it.

FIVE

CONFIDENCE GAMES

Walk tall and be considerate

◆

Confidence gets knocked out of you many times. Some-times you have to fake confidence by walking tall. It's a game. Good posture runs in my family. My mother was a dancer, my father was a chiropractor, and his mother was one of the first chiropractors in Canada. My siblings and I learned good posture early, and continued with my sisters, who became dancing teachers, and my brother Scott, who became a chiro-practor. We all walk upright.

My father hosted annual walking competitions in our front yard. I've never heard of anybody else hosting a competition like that. He was a great marketer! He would invite all his patients and their friends to the big garden in the front yard of his clinic. My mom would bake a lot of pies and freeze them. We had a huge freezer, big enough that she could feed pies to a thousand people. She also served coffee and tea. When all the guests were seated in the garden, the competition would start, with certificates offered for the best posture. Everyone looked confident and happy.

People have remarked on my posture all my life. Nowadays, people assume it comes from modeling, but that isn't it at all. It's from my family. If you see someone walking tall, don't you wish you could also walk like that? Yes, you can, if you practice. When you slouch, you look sad and insecure. When you walk tall, you look strong and confident. If you want to look and feel more confident, start with better posture. Stand up straight. Put your shoulders back, have a pleasant expression on your face, and look at people when they talk to you; don't look away. Call this your confidence game.

Besides posture, manners matter, too. I grew up with parents who were very quiet-spoken and well-mannered, maybe because they were Canadian. They were always polite and considerate of others. At modeling school, there was an etiquette class. And there, they taught us how to order at a restaurant and which knives and forks to use.

I've used what I learned about table manners all my life. When I taught students in my modeling school in Bloemfontein, South Africa, I had an etiquette class, too. It wasn't only for models; all the parents at the university and at the schools were sending their kids to me to teach them how to have good manners.

For all my models, part of my teaching was about showing

up on time, speaking clearly, and not being shy. When you have good manners, you are definitely more confident. You also appear more confident to other people. When I see someone with good manners, I appreciate him or her. And it's so easy to have good manners.

I've always wanted my children and my grandchildren to carry themselves proudly and politely, to have good posture and good manners, and I hope I set a good example for them, the way my parents did for me.

My son Elon has five boys. When I moved to LA, we would have family dinners, and it was just chaotic. You can imagine how noisy it got with everyone talking.

I said, "From now on, I'm going to spend thirty minutes alone with each boy each week." Friday afternoons, I went to their home. We sat and talked about their schoolwork and what they want to do and what they are interested in. Sometimes I just played a game with them or read them a book.

Then I took them to the table. I showed them how to eat politely. How to speak politely. How to wait until there is a time to speak and not shout over the other boys. "Eat with your mouth closed." "Don't talk with your mouth full." How to use their knife and fork properly. And they learned!

I said to them, "And when you're finished, you take your plate to the kitchen, but you also take your dad's plate and my plate. And instead of telling Dad what you've done for the day, ask him how his day was."

We all got together for dinner, and the kids behaved very nicely. Elon came in and sat down, and one of the boys said, "How was your day?"

He looked puzzled.

Another of his sons said, "I wanted to ask first!"

And the other one said, "No, I wanted to ask first!"

So that was quite funny.

Then they argued about taking his plate to the kitchen. I said it meant they have to take turns.

Today, years later, they are very polite kids, and I'm proud of them.

People are more receptive to you when you behave properly, and it's more impressive than being loud and rambunctious and jumping all around. It makes other people appreciate your company.

Even if you are a very confident person naturally, you will still gain and lose your confidence many times in your life. Hopefully, as you get older, you lose your confidence for a shorter time. In my seventies, you would think I would have less confidence. But my confidence is better than ever, because I am not worried about rejection or insults. As a model, I get rejected nine times out of ten. If you are losing confidence, you have to find a reason why you are losing your confidence. Many women aren't confident. They feel they have to be good at everything, they have been beaten down by people criticizing them, or they're taking on too much and cannot succeed at everything. Practice doing what you're good at, and don't try to be the best at everything.

As a child, I was good at schoolwork and terrible at sports, although I've tried every kind of sporting activity. My twin sister, Kaye, was not good at schoolwork but was a natural sports person. We were proud of each other and appreciated each other's accomplishments. We certainly didn't lose our confidence because we weren't good at both.

If you are usually confident, and then it goes away on a bad day, analyze why it's a bad day. What knocked the confidence out of you? Did someone make a remark that really hurt? Did they realize it hurt? Why are you so affected by that comment? Sometimes at work, you see other people are better at some aspects of the job that you would like to be good at. You should work harder at your talents and learn from those who are more experienced and better.

After my divorce, I regained confidence by having a happy home, raising happy children, making new friends who were kind to me, and becoming successful as a dietitian and a model.

You may need to make a big change to gain your confidence after you've lost it. Feeling down all the time is not a way to live. You need to surround yourself with family, friends, and colleagues who appreciate you for who you are. That will make you walk really tall and with confidence.

PART TWO

Adventure

SIX

JACARANDA SEASON

Go your own way

◆

Most people follow the norm. My father didn't. He was extraordinary. He wanted to fly around the world.

My father, Joshua Haldeman, loved to explore, and he was

not content with only driving, so I grew up with a Bellanca airplane as part of the family. It was made of canvas and had a propeller, and it was named Winnie, after my mother.

My mother's name was Winnifred; everybody called her Wyn. She was fabulous, and the older I got, the more I understood her brilliance.

Her parents had immigrated to Canada from England, and my mother grew up in a town called Moose Jaw. My father's family had emigrated from Switzerland to Philadelphia in 1727. He was born in Minnesota, and when he was four, his family moved to Waldeck, Saskatchewan, to live on a farm.

My parents met just after the Great Depression. The Canadian Depression was a terrible time, when people were lining up and begging for food and basic medical care for their children. Desperate to survive, they often leaned on the barter system. My dad had studied chiropractic medicine in Davenport, Iowa. He broke in horses in exchange for room and board, and gave chiropractic adjustments in exchange for food. My mother was only sixteen. She worked at the *Moose Jaw Times-Herald,* one of only two people left on staff, and she kept her job only because she was the lowest-paid staff member. Her family survived on her small weekly wage.

In her twenties, she trained to become a dancer and traveled to Chicago, New York, and Vancouver to study dance and dramatics. Can you imagine the long train journey she took as a single woman in that era? That is adventurous!

After the Depression, both of my parents moved to Regina, Saskatchewan, and opened businesses. My father opened a chiropractic practice. My mother started a dance school. I've got articles from local newspapers, along with photos of her dancing, and of the school, with all the students.

My father came for a ballroom dance lesson. He liked her very much and asked her out to dinner.

She said, "I don't date my clients." So he canceled his lessons and asked her to go to dinner again. She said yes.

In their wedding photo, they look very drab, because they didn't have any money. She's wearing a plain gray suit, and he's in a suit. She made all her own clothes and probably made her own wedding suit as well. Yet they were always happy, always smiling from the start.

My parents had four children in Regina. My father already had a son from a previous marriage, my brother Jerry, who looks so much like him. Then came my older brother Scott, my older sister Lynne, and in 1948, me and my twin, Kaye.

They got the Bellanca in 1948, the same year Kaye and I were born. The Bellanca was their second. The first, a Luscombe, was purchased when my parents were driving from Regina to Calgary. My father saw a plane sitting in a farmer's field with a FOR SALE sign. He did not have any cash, but he did have the car they were driving. So he exchanged the car for the plane, put my mother on a train back to Regina, and hired a pilot to fly him and the plane back to Regina.

Unfortunately, my father got airsick, probably from damage he had sustained to his inner ear from his days breaking horses during the Depression, and the pilot had to land on roads from time to time until he was ready to go back up. He never got airsick as long as he was the pilot in charge, but he felt uneasy when he was a passenger.

He was forty-four at the time.

My father used the planes regularly to get around Saskatchewan and Alberta. He flew all the way to LA once, but he had difficulty seeing the airport because of the smog. Navigational systems were not what they are today—far from it! Once, they had to follow a bush pilot to get back through the Rockies.

My first flight was at three months, when my parents flew me and my twin sister, Kaye, to a conference in Iowa. First, we stopped over in Edmonton. The only reason I know this is that there were photos of me and Kaye in the local papers. They called us the "flying twins."

My father was magnificent. He was fearless and adventurous, and we trusted him completely.

He was a great man who taught by example. He worked long hours, was thoughtful and kind. He was a gentle giant who never talked much. My kids don't remember meeting my dad, because he passed away when the boys were babies and I was pregnant with Tosca. All three whistle a lot, and I love it when they do. It reminds me of my father, who used to hum all the time. It makes me happy, because I have always thought you can only whistle or hum when you're happy.

In 1950, my parents decided to move away from Canada. They met missionaries who had been to South Africa, who had told them how beautiful it was. So they packed up the plane, the 1948 Cadillac, all of us and our belongings, and off we went on a cargo ship for two months to Africa. I don't know how my mom coped on the ship with two-year-old twins, and then two other children of six and eight. But she did.

My dad took the wings off the plane, because he always did his own work on his plane, put it in a crate, and shipped it to Cape Town. We all camped at the airport while Dad put the wings back on so that he could fly around and explore. The wood from those crates wound up becoming furniture for the clinic he would open when we settled in. Some of those bookcases lasted for decades.

My father wanted to live inland, so people suggested we fly to Johannesburg because they spoke English there. In nearby Pretoria, everybody spoke Afrikaans, and it would be much harder to settle in.

But when we flew over Pretoria, it was jacaranda time, and the whole city was covered in lilac blossoms.

He'd never seen anything so beautiful, and he said, "This is where we'll stay."

Pretoria was where we grew up, in a house with large trees (rare in the prairies of Saskatchewan) where people were warm. Afrikaaners called all adults Uncle and Auntie, Oom and Tannie, whether you knew them well or not. We thought that was cute.

In Canada, they thought we were crazy because my parents would fly around in their single-prop canvas plane with their small children; this was unheard of. Then we got to South Africa. There they thought we were even crazier. One person called us the "crazy Americans." (We were Canadian, of course, but it was all the same to them.)

People thought we were so weird because we did things our own way. It wasn't just because we were from somewhere else, because we had done things our own way back in Canada, too. We were different because of our travels; because our school uniforms were made by Mom, whereas other children had bought uniforms; because we had coffee brewing instead of tea; because our back door was always open for anyone to come and visit whereas other children's parents would arrange for someone to visit their children; and because we had brown bread sandwiches for school lunch and everyone else had white bread sandwiches. We were never given tuckshop money. I longed for those sausage rolls and Cornish pasties, but I rarely had one because I didn't want to spend my pocket money on it. We also had a Cadillac, which was the only Cadillac imported except for my dad's friend, who also then imported a Cadillac. And we had a plane. I didn't know anyone else with a plane, again other than my dad's friend.

My father was never one to do what anyone else was doing. When my dad felt he wanted to do something, he did it. So did my mother, who had created her own career and path before she even met my dad.

When I was five, they traveled by air from Pretoria to Oslo for a chiropractic conference, which took them through other parts of Africa, Spain, and France. They also stopped over in London so my dad could have a visit with some chiropractors he knew there.

When I was six, they began to plan for a trip to Australia, a round-trip journey of more than thirty thousand miles, because, of course, they had to fly themselves back. That was the norm for them; it was not the norm for our neighbors. Besides not being normal, our parents had to navigate with a compass, as there was no GPS and no radio. Their trips took a lot of planning, and they always planned ahead, because they knew that things can go wrong and they wanted to be ready. With no GPS, you needed to study the maps very carefully. With no radio, you had to be ready to rely on yourself. A trip of that distance requires a lot of fuel, so they had to remove the back seats of the plane to put in gas tanks, because when they crossed the sea to Australia, they would need to have extra gas. They brought tools they might need to repair anything on the plane, and my father knew how to repair his own plane.

My parents survived these trips by being very careful. By plane, they would check the weather, use a compass, navigate on a map, and then fly low over a town to read the signs to check that it was the right town to land in. Sometimes they would land on a sports field, or on a street, because there were no airports. They were braver than me. Now that I realize what they did, I'm surprised they survived.

Having a plan does not mean that things will go right. It means that if things go wrong, you will make another plan.

Their journey took them up the coast of Africa, across Asia, over the Pacific Ocean, and back again. We still have the maps that show the route they took, just my dad, my mom, and Winnie, flying over the Pacific in search of the world.

At that point, they had been to sixty countries. Every time they stopped somewhere, it was painted on the wing.

. . .

As children, we had to take responsibility for ourselves, which was unusual, even for the time.

Even when we were just four years old, my twin sister and I walked to school, holding hands. We would walk with my older sister, Lynne, who was seven, who helped us cross three roads over about half a mile. Our nursery school was a good three hundred yards farther than her school, so Kaye and I would walk the last bit by ourselves. And then we would walk back to Lynne's school and wait for her. She would walk us back again.

We were encouraged to be self-reliant.

My brother Scott remembers a trip he took with my parents. They flew through Central Africa, through Uganda, Kenya, Zanzibar, and Nairobi. Scott says that in Zanzibar and Nairobi, he was allowed to roam the streets by himself. As he says, today that would be considered child abuse! But for us it was completely normal.

On all our trips, we were expected to be capable. The first time I was on horseback, we were in what is today called Lesotho. It's a very mountainous region. The trip was sixty miles over the course of a few days. My younger brother Lee, who was born in Pretoria, was only five, and stayed behind with my mom. Scott was seventeen.

We spent long days in the saddle, and it was quite a rough trip, and wet. We never lit a fire and ate only canned food and bread. Sleep was limited, because at night, the cattle kept trying to lick our faces or steal our blankets.

Perhaps that's why it never bothered me to share a small

apartment with my children. A sofa bed is not the most comfortable, but it is much easier to get a good night's sleep indoors without a steer's tongue trying to lick the salt off your cheek.

You don't always have to follow what is expected of you. You can go your own way. I learned this lesson as a child and have used it in adulthood. After I got my dietetics degree and fell pregnant, I couldn't go looking for a job, so I started my private practice. This was frowned upon by my colleagues, as they said I should spend at least five years in a hospital before I start my own practice. I didn't have that option, and I really enjoyed helping people eat better. That would be the reason I could move around the world and start my nutrition practice all over again, again, and again. Moving is hell, but I guess I'm always willing to try something that could be fun or exciting.

If you are doing the same thing every day of your life, staying in the same job, living in the same place, and you are happy, you can stay that way.

If you are restless or unhappy, and want to make a change, start researching what you can do, where you can live, and what job would be the most satisfying for you. Learning about new places and mixing with new people can broaden your mind and make you happier.

My father always said, "There's nothing a Haldeman can't do." And that is what I have always believed, and my siblings, too. I have probably shown that to my own children. Now there's nothing a Musk can't do.

SEVEN

EXPLORATION

Plan for the expected, and be ready for the unexpected

◆

E very July, which was winter in South Africa, my family went out in search of the lost city of the Kalahari. At the time, Botswana was called Bechuanaland. Sometimes my dad would take the plane and my mom would drive the car. Other times we would all go by truck, with a compass, and spend three weeks crossing the Kalahari Desert. My mom packed the car with three weeks' supply of food, water, and gas, as well as five children.

My dad got the idea to look for the lost city from a book written by Guillermo Farini, a Canadian who crossed the desert in the late nineteenth century in an ox wagon. He said that he had found the ruins of a lost city. Farini is also known for walking over Niagara Falls on a tightrope, so you know that he was always up for an adventure.

My father wanted to try to follow Farini's path by car, and that became our July vacations. Now I think: Can you imagine taking five little kids to the desert for three weeks? My mom didn't have to go, of course. She had a choice. She could have stayed at home with the kids. But he was going to go anyway, and she didn't want to leave him alone, so we all went together.

I was never afraid on my trips to the desert, because my dad and mom were in charge. Even when I was told a hyena could bite off my face, I just closed my sleeping bag so that the hyena couldn't. I didn't assume anything could go wrong on these trips. Perhaps my parents discussed safety, because they were always prepared. They seemed to figure out everything. I didn't think about the packing, because my mom would take care of it. Looking back, she had to think about every detail: clothes, food, water for all five of us kids. My dad had to think of maps, the compass, gas, car repair tools. They were quite amazing.

Everything was considered in advance. We had to bring a three-week supply of water. We'd bring canned vegetables and canned fruit. We had enough fresh food for the first week, but not much longer, and then, of course, you couldn't get anymore.

This was where our family motto of "live dangerously— carefully" was put to its test. Of course things could go wrong. So you thought in advance about what that could be and you planned for it.

We knew it was possible to get lost. We would see the grave-stones of people who had died in the desert. My father some-times hired guides who translated for us, but there were so many different tribes, and they all spoke different languages, so usu-ally we were on our own. There were camel patrols who worked with the Bechuanaland government, since Botswana was con-trolled by the British. My parents would plan to start in one tiny town and end in another, and the camel patrols knew we were there and when to expect us. They were always ready to come looking for us if we didn't reach the other side in three weeks.

My dad knew we would get stuck in the sand, so he packed shovels. When we were stuck, we dug ourselves out. To avoid potholes in the bush, us kids took turns running ahead of the car, to make sure there were no holes or stumps, because there was no road. And we had the tools so that my dad could repair any problems with the truck. He had a welding iron, so when the car once did hit a tree stump, my dad and my older brother Scott made a fire to heat the welding iron, and fit it back to-gether so that we could continue our journey.

Things broke. We didn't panic. We fixed them and carried on. In life, we fear many things that don't happen. When bad things happen, we need to find a solution. Once, petrol got into the drinking water, and we drank petrol water, because there was nothing else to do. As soon as we could, we got fresh water, and that was that.

Every day, we woke at dawn, packed up, and drove until near darkness, then made camp. We had a tent that housed the food supplies.

We all had chores. Kaye and I gathered dry wood, and my brother made a fire. My mother mixed water, powdered eggs, powdered milk, flour, and baking powder, and baked us scones in a big iron pot. In the middle of the desert, we ate fresh, warm scones. Can you imagine the planning it took to make that possible? As an adult I think about all the work that my mother did in advance, to make it so delicious for us.

My dad had a license to shoot one animal per week, for the pot. We shot a buck or a guinea fowl, and when we had enough food for us, we gave the rest to whatever tribe we came across. We all had shooting lessons in the desert, too. My mother was a champion shot.

Everything we needed, we brought with us. Kaye and I had one bowl of water to wash in at night and in the morning. In the desert, it got so cold at night that the water turned to ice, and we had to break up the ice to wash our hands and faces in the morning.

We learned to live without all the comforts of home. When that's what you have to do, it's what you do.

We went to the toilet behind a bush. We went without showers. That was okay, because it's the desert, and sand isn't

dirty. While our parents mapped our next course, we children read a lot. I have photos of all of us reading, our faces tucked into our books.

I certainly learned that I don't need comfort. You can do with very little.

This was where I learned that you can always cut back on expenses; don't go into debt, don't envy other people who live in luxury—just do the best you can, strive to survive, and then hopefully be successful.

One winter, we had a guide named Hendrik. Hendrik slept by the fire, which he told us was the safest spot, because no animal would come near a fire.

But one evening, my father lit the paraffin lamp that was on the table and saw that there was a lion, right there in the camp. He slowly backed up to the tent and said, "Wyn, a lion. Pass me my torch and gun." (He always called a torch a torch and not a flashlight. We had to adjust our use of the word when we got to Canada.)

The lion wandered over to Hendrik, who was by the fire. Unfortunately, the lion had not read the rules. He didn't know that he wasn't supposed to get near the fire.

My father called out, "Hendrik, a lion!"

Hendrik jumped straight out of his blankets and over the fire and shouted, "*Voetsek*," which means, "Go away!" The lion wandered slowly out of the camp as my father fired a couple of shots over his head, but he didn't react. The lion's mate was waiting just outside the camp. My father got into the car to chase them away, and the lions made their way up the sand dune next to the camp and then spent the morning watching us.

My brother Lee remembers that he was sent to sleep in the car. He was the littlest, and as he was the tastiest morsel in the camp, we had to keep him safe.

My father didn't seem scared; if he was, we didn't know it. His attitude made us feel safe.

We saw lots of animals and insects on those journeys: springbok, wildebeest, lizards, anthills, vultures, and other birds of prey. Once, a scorpion bit my mom and we had to use a tourniquet and suck out the blood. Once, an ostrich chased Lynne. We found that funny. Then of course there were the hyenas. We were scared of those! Hyenas are quite vicious.

I remember one morning when Scott and I went walking along the Okavango River and he shot a guinea fowl for us to eat. It fell into the river. Scott sent me to swim in to fetch it.

When I came out, I stood on something that moved. It was a crocodile. We had no idea the river was full of crocodiles. It was very startling, but I'm still here, so it all turned out all right.

I know that my dad wanted to find that lost city, but we never did. He went back twelve times. I was there for eight of those trips. I wasn't disappointed that we didn't find the lost city, because my parents didn't express disappointment. We had a lot of adventures and had fun times together as a family.

You can aim for a goal, but if it doesn't work out, that's okay.

I think my father just loved to explore the unknown, learn about new cultures, and discover new areas; he and my mom never stopped learning. He loved bush-bashing, making his own roads through the desert. He always went according to the compass. We never got lost; we always came out where he wanted to be.

EIGHT

WHY NOT?

Say yes to opportunities

◆

I had a plan for my career: I was going to study science. I thought about medicine, or microbiology, or biochemistry. My dad encouraged me to do a degree that would qualify me to graduate in four years with a profession. I decided to study dietetics.

In my third year, one of my fellow students said, "I'm going to nominate you for Vaal Queen."

I said, "What is that?"

That's how much I knew.

He explained that it was a beauty competition. I had never gone out for a pageant. I told him that I was a nerd, not a beauty queen.

For a laugh, he put me up for it, and I was chosen to enter. I wasn't sure if I should do it, because it wasn't my kind of thing. I said yes anyway. Why not, right? It wasn't going to mean anything in the long run.

I thought it was a silly afternoon that I probably would never remember. But it changed my life.

I am really glad I participated in the beauty competition. It introduced me to a more professional modeling agency in Johannesburg. Surprisingly, this became a lifelong second career for me.

Before I arrived at the building where the pageant was held, I had no idea how seriously some women took a pageant like that. I was just a student, remember, and I had not had the experience to know that for a competition, you're meant to spend time and money preparing to win that crown. The other girls looked magnificent. They had obviously had their hair done, and their makeup was very professional. And so were their swimsuits.

I was wearing my own swimsuit and did my own hair and makeup. My whole family came, which was surprising. It wasn't the sort of thing they'd usually come out for, but they did.

Backstage, they gave us numbers.

"I don't want to be number one," said the girl who had been chosen to go first.

I said, "I'll take it." I wasn't afraid. Not because I was confident but because I couldn't care less about walking that runway. I had my exams to think about, and I had a boyfriend who had just cheated on me. There were bigger things. We all walked. At the end, Kaye was crying, saying, "You were the best."

I said, "Yeah, right."

But I won! I was elated.

Some of the girls were really upset because they had been depending on a win to promote their modeling career. I was happy to win, but I thought the experience was just something for fun. The prizes included 100 rand (about $150), a contract with a Johannesburg modeling agency, and fees for a modeling course in Johannesburg.

They also gave me ten bowling tickets.

Funny enough, after I'd won and everyone had finished taking photos, there was no party. We just had to leave. So my family went bowling using my tickets. That was lovely. I hadn't imagined any of that. Nor could I foresee that starting that modeling course would lead to photo shoots in Johannesburg, which is only thirty miles from Pretoria. It was the main center for modeling. I started driving there in my sister's car. That is where I learned proper modeling techniques and professionalism.

Saying yes to modeling and to pursuing my degree were two completely separate entities. My main focus for most of my life was studying nutrition and running my own business as a dietitian. I never depended on modeling as a source of income. When I modeled, it was definitely a bonus, but I did it because it was fun, kept me in the fashion world, and allowed me to meet very creative people.

My modeling career has done so much for me. Modeling has given me a completely different group of colleagues and friends who I wouldn't have known if I just remained a dietitian and mixed with scientists. Also, modeling helped me explore the world, each city, because castings can be anywhere, and photo shoots can be either in dreadful or fabulous locations.

Now, I don't think that much before saying yes. I'll say yes if I'm curious, if it could be interesting or fun or improve my circumstances.

If you would like to make changes, you need to say, "Why not?"

At the time, the modeling competition seemed like a small "why not?" But sometimes, that can be the right attitude for even very big life changes.

When Tosca was thirty-seven, she decided it was time to have children. She had been focused on her life and career, and the idea of children was always on the back burner. But she began feeling that her chances of having children were getting slimmer by the day, and she wasn't going to settle for a relationship with someone just to have children. She told us she wanted to do IVF and have kids by herself, and our family supported the idea.

Of course there were people who told her not to have children by herself. They told her that it would be too hard to do alone, that it wasn't going to be the right choice, or that it would hurt her career or be bad for the kids. But those people were just scared for themselves. What other people, unrelated to you, think you should do with your life is not something to base your decisions on. Of course, having children is a big life change no matter what your situation.

I remember just saying: Go for it! I'll help you choose the sperm donor! I also told her that it was so much easier without a man involved—something she agrees with to this day. I was with her through all the tests (a lot of tests) and disappointments (heartbreaking at times), and it was tough. As Tosca had to lie down for four days after her eggs were implanted, I flew in from New York. It was also the week she was moving. While she watched *The West Wing* on the couch, I sorted through all her belongings and filled twelve large bags for thrift stores or the dumpster. On her thirty-eighth birthday, she found out that both embryos had taken and she was pregnant. The pregnancy wasn't easy either, but pregnancies are not that easy. And now she has two beautiful children who light up our lives (and challenge us) daily. All women who do IVF deserve a big round of applause. It is difficult, but it's worth it.

Tosca says that it's the best decision she has made in her life. Her children ground her and are a source of such unconditional love. She tells me they make her look at the world in a completely different way—how can she make it better for them? What is she doing to help them? It humbles and inspires her.

It's complicated with work, as she travels all over the world to make movies, but they get to be together and experience new places in the world and see their mother working hard (just like my children saw me working hard). And I get to babysit them.

No matter how big or small the opportunity, someone else will always answer the question for you of "why not?" But think about what's going to make *you* happy. Keep opening doors for yourself in your life; you just never know until you try.

NINE

A WOMAN MAKES A PLAN

Take charge of your own life, and aim for happiness

◆

G rowing up in our family, we always had kindness and consideration around us. Once we got out in the world, we had a reality check. My siblings and I joke that it wasn't until we left home that we learned how awful people can be! I trusted that everybody had goodness in them. Consequently, I suffered. It took a long time for me to learn how to protect myself, unfortunately.

I went to university in Pretoria, the town where my family lived. I grew up with North American parents and we spoke English at home, but the dietetics degree I wanted to do was only offered at an Afrikaans university. All the classes, everything, was in Afrikaans. Due to the language gap, I had to work harder than everybody else just to keep up, and it didn't help with making friends either.

But I did have an on-and-off boyfriend since I was sixteen. He was good at math and science, better than me, and I didn't know many guys like that. And he kept saying that he wanted to marry me.

When I found out that he was cheating on me with another girl, I became so upset that I couldn't eat. I cried for a week. Because of grief, I dropped ten pounds. That was when I did the Vaal Queen competition, which gave me professional training to be a model and a contract and a whole other life outside of school. I was going to Johannesburg to model and doing quite well. I became Miss LM Radio, which was the coolest radio station that played the top 20 hits.

I was a finalist for Miss South Africa. I thought if I won, I could stop university, as I was so tired of studying in Afrikaans. In my final year of university, the stress was constant. I did not realize just how hard it would be to study physics and chemistry in a language that was not my native tongue. To make myself feel better, I ate. I ate so much that by the time I graduated, I weighed 205 pounds. Fortunately, I didn't win Miss South Africa.

I started interviewing for jobs, and I was either overqualified or underqualified for everything that interested me. At one interview, for a position I was deemed wrong for, I got an introduction to someone who had a food company that was looking for a nutritional expert in Cape Town. So I took the job and moved. I was twenty-one.

My on-and-off boyfriend, who I hadn't seen for a year, came down to visit me with an engagement ring. He said that he was in love with me and that he would be good to me from then on. He would change if I married him.

I said no. I would never wear his ring.

He went back to Pretoria and told my parents that I'd agreed to marry him. They were very surprised, as they didn't know we were dating. As we weren't.

Back at home, Kaye and her boyfriend had been dating for a long time, and they were getting ready to get married. My dad suggested we make it a double wedding. Everybody thought it was a wonderful idea! They organized the wedding, printed out the wedding invitations, and sent them out. Gifts were arriving.

I learned about all of this in a telegram. It read, "Congratulations!" This was the first news I had of my engagement. I was shocked. The telegram went on to say that I needed to quit my job and come back home, because the wedding was going to be in one month.

This may sound strange to modern ears, but you've got to understand that this was 1970, in South Africa, where we didn't make long-distance phone calls. They were too expensive. We sent telegrams or we visited in person. And men would often approach a woman's father to ask for her hand. So to my father, none of this seemed strange, as he was told I'd agreed to marry my ex-boyfriend.

Well, he sure timed it right. I was lonely, and I had thrown out my back and was in pain. I did not have any confidence because of all the weight I had gained. I hated the way that I looked, and I thought that no man would want to date me. I did what the telegram said, quit my job, and packed up my things and flew home.

In Pretoria, I saw my boyfriend had not changed. He was still very aggressive. I didn't know what to do about the wedding. We were a close family, but we didn't talk a lot about our feelings. All around me, people were preparing for the wedding. My older sister, Lynne, was making a wedding dress for me, with plenty of chiffon so that my figure was concealed. In a few weeks' time, eight hundred people were set to arrive. All my parents' friends, my twin sister's friends, her fiancé's friends. And my and his friends. I couldn't see a way out of getting married. There was no escaping it, in my mind.

We had a double wedding. What I remember is that Kaye and her new husband were so happy. My new husband was just furious about the fact that their happiness took the limelight from him.

Then came the years when my life was hell. It's not a time in my life that I like to talk about, because it is so painful. It makes me angry and bitter. That is not what I want to be. After I talk about it, I toss and turn at night. I can't sleep. Yet it would be an untruth to suggest or pretend that life is easy. Life is most certainly not easy. It can be brutal and unrelenting. When it is, you have to get yourself out. Please. Do it as quickly as you can.

I was hurt by men, went through slumps, and lost my confidence multiple times in my life. Each time I couldn't see a way out. And yet each time I found a way through the dark tunnel. It's not because I am especially fierce. I have been called that, but I don't think I am a fierce person. I do think I am strong, yet there were many times when I didn't feel strong. It took time to pull myself out. But I did, eventually. I'm telling you this story, which isn't even as bad as other women's stories, so that you can know that you can get out of bad situations. I offer my story to you as proof that you, too, can find the inspiration and confidence to make a change and find a happier life. We all deserve a happy life.

Right away, I found out that my job as a wife was to do everything. We flew to Europe the night of our wedding, on my savings. We took a really cheap flight and stayed with his cousin in Geneva to save some money. It was the time when you could travel Europe on $5 a day, and that was our goal.

I had to unpack everything, I had to pack everything. I had to cook for him. I had to clean up while he sat and read *Playboy*. *Playboy* was banned in South Africa, so he was happy they weren't banned in Europe.

It was on our honeymoon that he hit me for the first time. I was shocked when he started beating me up. I wanted to leave, but I couldn't, because he had my passport.

When we got home, I thought of going to my family to say, "You were right. He's a monster." But I was too embarrassed. Soon after, I started getting very nauseated from morning sickness, and I realized I was pregnant. I had conceived on the second day of our honeymoon. It was so clear that marrying him had been a mistake, but now it was really impossible to undo.

He was cruel in ways that didn't make sense. Just before I had Elon, he was repainting his plane, and I was helping him. Every time I had a contraction, I had to slow down. And he'd say, "You don't have to slow down when you have contractions."

He refused to take me to the hospital until the contractions were five minutes apart.

He said, "You're just being lazy and weak."

Then when I was in hospital, I had a natural childbirth, and I was in great pain.

The nurse said to my husband, "Just rub her back. It'll make her feel better."

He said, "What do you mean? She should rub my back. Look at the stool you gave me to sit on. I'm leaving. You can call me five minutes before she's giving birth."

That's the kind of man he was.

I was very busy in my early twenties. In the mornings, I worked for my husband, typing his engineering specifications and doing his accounting. I had a small private nutrition practice at my apartment. After Elon, I had Kimbal and Tosca, three births in three years and three weeks. Along with all this, it was my job to take care of the children, and the house, and to cook, and to clean.

My parents had allowed us to build a house on a plot of land just next to theirs, so we did. I had a little truck that I had bought with my savings, and I filled it with bricks, cement, and timber and then drove the hour to the plot.

The kids would be rolling around on the seat next to me, because we didn't have seat belts in those days. My father's builder was helping to build this home.

I remember being very pregnant while tiling the bathroom walls.

When the house was completed, we stayed there on weekends.

. . .

I was pregnant with Tosca when my father died in a plane crash. He was flying with Kaye's husband, my brother-in-law, and neither of them survived.

My husband wanted to know how much money we would get from my dad's death.

I said, "Well, I don't think we get anything. I think my mom gets everything."

He said, "That's not right. I didn't marry you just so your mother would get the money."

Meanwhile, my mom gave us my dad's plane and sold us the plot where we had built our house at a very low cost.

He was still furious, because he wanted more.

Sometime later, Kaye remarried. Her husband was a chiropractor, and Kaye bought my dad's clinic, which was next door to her house. But my husband thought that she had gotten more than me, and he became incensed.

He wouldn't let me speak to my family for two years. They weren't allowed to see my kids. Every time my mom phoned, I would quickly say goodbye and put down the phone.

He would say, "It's a man. It's a man calling you." And then he'd beat me up.

It wasn't a man. It was my mom. If I'd said that, he would have beaten me up for that, too.

He cut me off from my family. It was a terrible time.

As my husband's business did better, he bought more cars, a plane, and a boat. Showing his wealth was all he cared about.

Throughout my marriage, I was told many times a day that I was boring, stupid, and ugly. I thought, "Well, I can't help that I'm boring. But I can't be that stupid if I have a Bachelor of Science degree. And I can't be that ugly if I've won beauty titles and modeled." I never said any of that. If I had said that, I would have been beaten up.

But sometimes, he would say, "I know what you're thinking," and he'd beat me up for that, too.

In my mid-twenties, I read the book *I'm OK—You're OK*. It gave me strength and hope. He wanted to take the book away from me. He didn't like me reading that book at all.

Occasionally we would have people over for dinner. Every meal had to be prepared from scratch, including baking the bread. I don't like cooking, but I had recipe books. I would follow them to the letter, and the dishes would be amazing.

He would speak to me in the nastiest way and insult me in front of our guests, and they would never come back. When they didn't return, he would say, "See, your food wasn't good enough, and you're boring. That's why they won't come back."

After I had my kids, I wasn't modeling anymore. I didn't think I would ever go back to modeling. Even if I had been asked to go back to modeling, I really couldn't, because of my bruises.

We were at an Oktoberfest celebration with three other couples, and everybody was drinking beer and having fun, and some of the people were a little drunk. The three other ladies were gorgeous women. I was dressing so conservatively you wouldn't believe it, and the women I was with were dressed up, very cool.

We all stood to go to the bathroom, and so the guys at the table next to us whistled and said, "Hey, beautiful, you're all so sexy," or something like that.

My husband screamed at me and called me a slut. He lunged at me to hit me, in front of everybody.

He'd lost it. Over time, he had gotten crazier. At the beginning, he would only hit me in my home. Now the abuse was so bad that he was willing to do it in public.

My friends' husbands grabbed him off me, and the wives grabbed me and took me to my mom's. She was surprised to see me at 2:00 a.m., knocking on the window, as she hadn't seen me for two years.

The next morning he came to her home. He begged my mom to send me back to him. He cried and apologized.

My mom said, "Never touch her again, or she's coming back here." She was furious that he'd been hitting me. She also didn't know why I didn't tell her about my terrible marriage. I think I was embarrassed. And I was scared he would hurt my family.

Well, he listened to my mom and never hit me again after that. Before, he would hit me when the kids were around. I remember that Tosca and Kimbal, who were two and four, respectively, would cry in the corner, and Elon, who was five, would hit him on the backs of his knees to try to stop him. I was relieved that he stopped when they were young enough that they might not remember. Then, I only had to tolerate his verbal abuse. When the physical abuse stopped, the verbal abuse got worse; however, I was free from pain and bruises.

. . .

Lettie called and asked if I was available to model. Now that I didn't have bruises, I could say yes. He was furious about that. He followed me to one show and stood behind a pillar and stared at me while I was working. He came backstage and saw the hairstylist working on my hair. He wanted to beat the guy up for touching my hair. He wanted to control everything that I did.

He said that if I ever divorced him, he would cut up my face with razor blades, and he would shoot the kids in the knees so that I'd have three crippled kids to bring up, and I wouldn't be able to work as a model. It was terrifying. I didn't divorce him sooner because I was scared.

I also didn't know that I could get out. I didn't have a case. The South African laws at the time were not in my favor, and there was no legal reason for me to get divorced. A man abusing a woman was not a reason for divorce. In fact, that's what men did, because that's what makes them a man, or that's what I had been led to believe.

The year they passed the laws for "irretrievable breakdown of marriage" was when I said, "I can get divorced now." Suddenly, there was a chance for me to get out.

I had to decide where to go. I could have stayed with my mom, but I thought she would be in danger. I didn't want him to come after her. We had sold the house next to my parents' weekend home and bought a holiday house near Durban in the middle of nowhere. That's where I went with my children.

I was lucky to have that option. His lawyer had suggested to put the Durban house in my name.

He said to the lawyer, "No. Nothing goes into her name."

The lawyer pointed out that he had a home, a yacht, a plane, six cars. Everything was in his name. If anything went wrong and people sued him, he could lose everything.

I said, "I don't care. Put it in his name."

He said, "Are you sure that you want it in my name?"

I said, "Yes, you can have it."

He said, "Okay, put it in her name."

As soon as it was in my name, I felt something relax inside me. We put down the money for the deposit, and then there was a mortgage of $300 a month.

I was an advantaged person. When the laws changed, I had a place to go with my kids. That's part of why I was able to leave.

I was confident about paying the mortgage because I had some savings. He had not had any money when he married me, but he did well as an engineer, and now he was very well off. He had quite a lot in his savings, and I had not very much in mine. But I felt it was enough money to feed my kids and pay my mortgage, at least for the first few months.

I was scared of my husband the whole time I was married. While I was getting divorced, I was scared of him the whole time, too.

While I was waiting for my divorce, he came to my home in Durban and chased me through the streets with a knife.

I ran into my neighbor's home, and she was in the kitchen.

She said, "Go into the garden; I have my friends there."

He ran in with the knife and said, "I want my wife."

She said, "Would you like a cup of tea?"

Later she said she was in such a state of shock that she didn't know what else to say.

But whatever she did worked. He fell on the floor crying, saying that he wanted me back.

She was terrified. So was I. After that, I got a restraining order against him.

All I wanted was to be free of him, and I had two lawyers who were also my patients. One was a vicious divorce lawyer, and the other one was a real estate lawyer. I went with the real estate lawyer. I didn't want a drawn-out case. I wanted it to be over. I didn't want his money. I didn't want anything but my children.

I got dressed to go to court in a red miniskirt, a white

 blouse, and red high-heeled shoes, and I did my hair and makeup fabulously. My mom took one look at me and said, "Wash your makeup off, tie your hair back, and wear some of your sister's old clothes and flat shoes."

I wore this flowery dress that was too big for me and went to the courthouse looking very plain.

The judge smiled and flirted with me.

He said, "Does your husband really want to divorce you?"

I said, "He signed the papers."

I couldn't lie and say he did want to. He didn't want to. But he had signed.

I asked for nothing except the kids, but the judge ruled that he had to give me 5 percent of his income and pay for their schooling, medical, and dental expenses, which he never did. The judge ruled that he had to give me a four-door car because of the kids. He had five luxury cars and my truck, but he went and found the cheapest car he could find, a Toyota Corolla with roll-up windows and no air-conditioning. Then he offered me a Jaguar or a Mercedes, on the condition that he would have to inspect it every month.

It was another way of trying to control me, so I chose the Toyota. It was good enough, it would get me where I needed to go, and he would not be involved.

I was happy to have a car that belonged to me.

I started my practice right away. In South Africa, dietetics was valued, and doctors in Durban were happy to send their patients to me. I was getting modeling jobs, too.

I always struggled with money, just to pay that mortgage. The kids had school uniforms, which were cheaper than regular clothes. I didn't buy myself nice clothes, or any clothes for that matter, and if I did, I got them secondhand.

One weekend a month, those first few years, the kids would go to him and I would pack their clothes. He would send them back without any clothes or bags, so I had to buy them new clothes every time. That was very upsetting, because I couldn't afford it.

It was all on purpose. He often said that I would eventually return to him, because I would be so poverty-stricken and wouldn't be able to feed them. For the next ten years, he sued me repeatedly for custody of the kids. It cost me all my savings, but I didn't have to put up with him twenty-four hours a day. Even though the court cases, all the preparation, and the fear of losing my kids was horrific, it was still better than living in constant fear.

I never went back. No matter how hard it is, you have to get through it. You have to get out. It's worth it.

If you are living in fear or dread of another person, you have to make a plan to get out of it. If you find yourself in an unhappy relationship, do everything you can to leave. I stayed too long, hoping that other people would change or that the situation would change. But nothing changed until I made a change.

When you do leave a relationship, you may find that it gets harder before it gets easier. You may have extreme loneliness afterward, and you will have to tolerate that. When you feel that loneliness, go visit your friends. Phone your family. Get a new job. See a movie. Move to another city.

A good plan needs to cover finances and logistics. You may need to ask for help, from friends and from professionals. There will be different stresses—financial, social—but I found I had many friends coming out of the woodwork who had avoided me because of my husband. Some couples even offered to help me financially, though I never accepted it.

. . .

Your plan doesn't need to be a five-year plan. If you're always thinking too far ahead, it can become too difficult to make that first step. The most important thing is to get out. Don't focus on the distant future. Focus on your next move.

When you realize that it's time to leave, the important thing is not to become overwhelmed by everything that will happen after. Plan that first step and then make another plan.

When I think about every bad situation I've been in, I can see now that I should have gotten out earlier. That moment, when you realize a situation is not a good situation, and it's not going to change: that's when you have to decide to get out of it. As soon as you can.

If your relationship is unhappy, what do you have to lose by breaking up? If you cannot change your partner, and you've tried, then there is no reason to remain unhappy for the rest of your life.

I was very lonely after my divorce, especially when my children went to their father for a weekend or on a vacation. He took them skiing in Austria, or to Hong Kong and New York. I didn't want to deprive the kids of these experiences. He always invited me, and I love traveling to new countries, but I always remembered how terrible it was to travel with him. He sucked the fun out of every situation.

Being lonely is better than living in fear in your relationship. Being unhappy is far worse. Loneliness never made me want to return to my unhappy marriage. Struggling financially is much better than being abused every day. I don't need the mansion, fancy clothes, cars, planes, boats, farms that came with daily misery.

So we lived in a small apartment, more than once. So my children and I ate a lot of peanut butter sandwiches. So we had a lot of bean soup. So what?

We loved each other. We had a lot of fun together. That's what matters.

I am telling you my story because if you are in a dark situation, I want you to know that there is a way out of it. I want you to know that if you are in a relationship with someone who is hurting you, you have to get out if you want to survive. For nine years I suffered in an abusive marriage. Once I left, I felt as if a dark cloud had been lifted and there was hope.

No matter how bleak it may seem, there is always another way.

TEN

TURN YOUR LIFE AROUND

Address your problems

◆

During my marriage, my weight went up and down. I got pregnant on my honeymoon, and I got morning sickness, which for me was really all-day sickness. First I lost too much weight. Then I gained too much weight. With every child, up and down. I was lucky that I had such healthy children. I wanted them to stay that way. I was feeding my kids so healthily and making their food.

Those years were the hardest of my life. My children are the best thing I ever did, but the marriage was a mistake. After I divorced and was living in Durban, a single mother of three young children, it was up to me to take care of us. It was crucial that I kept my weight down so that I could continue modeling and have extra income to support my kids. I relied on everything I knew about nutrition, eating only when I was hungry and only eating healthy foods: cereal, milk, vegetables, fruit, whole wheat peanut butter sandwiches, bean soup, canned fish, and sometimes chicken. What made it easier was that I had to keep to a low-budget diet anyway, and healthy food does not need to be expensive.

I made an effort to socialize in Durban, but my family was never impressed by any of my boyfriends. Kaye called me a jerk magnet, and she was right. While out one evening, I met a man who really liked me, and we fell into a relationship. He wanted me to lose weight, because he thought I looked fat. I wasn't fat, but I lost weight to please him. It was really stressful for me to get so thin. It was restrictive.

He asked me to marry him, but I said no, as he was cheating on me. He organized a surprise engagement party for me anyway. I guess I have a type. He was building a house to live in with me, with bedrooms for his and my children, plus a separate office and waiting room for my nutrition practice. Every time I tried to give him back his ring, he threatened suicide. I started eating three desserts every time he saw me to scare him away. I gained weight rapidly.

I loved eating fried, fatty, sweet foods, but I was eating them out of unhappiness and stress. I was back to 205 pounds. It took only a few months to put the weight back on, but it would take nearly ten years for me to get back to being a healthy size eight. Of course I didn't know that then.

I needed to figure out what to do next—a new plan. Planning felt impossible until one of my friends came to my rescue. Her advice was simple. She told me to spend half an hour every day remembering happy times and suggested that it would help me decide what to do next.

I had never meditated or spent any time just sitting and thinking. But my friend said I had to do that. It was very bizarre for me. So I sat for thirty minutes, and there'd be nothing in my brain. I mean, just nothing. Just trying to remember when I was happy. I was so sad, I couldn't remember any time I was happy. I thought, "Well, high school was fun," but I wasn't going back to high school. I realized that some of my happiest times had been at university, despite the stress of studying in Afrikaans. The benefit was that my Afrikaans was much better now!

That's when I decided to go to Bloemfontein to take my dietetic internship. I gave up everything and moved, along with my young children, from this lovely home in Durban to a small town in the middle of the country where everybody spoke Afrikaans.

I was just so sad that I said, "It's worth the move."

There was no social life for a divorced mother with young children in a small town, but I was completely absorbed in my studies. I lived with my children in the doctors' quarters. My kids were in the bedroom, and I slept in the living room/kitchen. It was all worth it, because when we got there, I was so happy to be away from that sadness. Not being in a place where I was constantly reminded of my pain made a big difference.

I volunteered my expertise teaching modeling and image

building in order to raise funds for scholarships for the dietetics program. It went so well that the students I had taught convinced me to run a school. This new venture became very successful. Professors' children, colleagues, friends, and the press all supported me. I produced fashion shows, lectured on nutrition and confidence, and had great fun. I even stayed on to get a Master of Science degree. What a way to build up my own self-esteem!

Life was good. I taught at night, so that became my social life. And in this university town, nobody judged me regarding my weight, which made me feel much more relaxed. I even dated a few cute guys who were younger than me.

I wanted to support the careers of the models I was training, so I went to Johannesburg, to the top modeling agency, G3, to show their photos.

The agent I met with was Gaenor Becker. She was not interested in any of my models. She sized me up and said, "What about you modeling?"

I said, "No, no, I don't model anymore."

I had lost perhaps twenty pounds over the months, but I wasn't thinking about my own modeling career.

Gaenor said that plus-size modeling was a new category, and she encouraged me to take it up, because I had the experience.

Once again, I helped myself greatly in the long run by saying, "Why not?"

My plus-size modeling career began with flying to Johannesburg to do TV commercials. As I was the only plus-size model in South Africa, I was soon traveling the country, doing print and runway shows while finishing my Master of Science degree. They needed one plus-size model and one older model, and I did both.

In the meantime, Gaenor and I had become good friends. After I moved to Johannesburg, Gaenor said to me, "I know the most dreadful man called Musk."

I said, "That must be my ex-husband."

She said, "He married my friend and kicked her out right after the wedding."

I said, "That would be him."

A couple of years after that, she said, "Do you want to meet Sue Musk?"

And I said, "Sure."

Sue was a top model, a beautiful woman, much cooler than me. We went to a cocktail party. She would introduce me to people and say, "This is Maye Musk. She married my ex for ten years and I married him for ten minutes."

We would laugh so much. People couldn't understand the joke, but we didn't care. We just laughed through it all.

In Johannesburg I was still doing my nutrition work, and my practice had expanded so much that I was giving talks about healthy eating. At the same time, I was medically obese, and so I masked my feelings about it with humor. I tried to make it funny, so that I would appear to be more confident—but I wasn't feeling very confident, and I was wearing large clothes to hide my body. Yet my clients were still coming to me and getting motivated. It made me feel like a fraud, because I was doing the opposite of what I was telling my clients to do. I had the information, but I wasn't using it myself.

At forty-one, my cholesterol had increased, and my knees and back were hurting. That was frightening, because you have to stay in good health when you have three kids to support. I missed feeling good in my body.

So I started taking my own advice: eating only when hungry, eating healthy foods, not overeating. When I took my own advice, I lost weight. This time I've kept it off for thirty years.

I want you to know that I work at it every day. It is not easy.

As someone who isn't naturally lean, if I want to keep my figure, I need to stay focused all day, every day. I'm always planning my meals and making sure there is healthy food around. If I don't eat enough, I don't feel my best. If I let myself get too hungry, I'll devour anything in sight. If I eat unhealthy foods, I can feel myself slow down mentally and physically and get tired and bloated. Even though I've been a dietitian for forty years, I can still be tempted and suffer for it. But most of the time, I'm making choices, again and again, to eat well, because I want to feel fantastic.

Pretty photographs don't show you all the work it takes to get there—I have gained and lost sixty-five pounds twice. I am fully aware that if I overeat, my weight will increase until I stop overeating. I really thought it would stay constant at some stage. It didn't. And it took a lot of effort to lose the weight. It still does.

. . .

It's easy to reach for an immediate solution to feeling bad, as I did with overeating. But that keeps you from facing the problem, and it will probably make you feel worse. If you want to feel better, you must turn it around and make a real change. Whether that is a small change, like learning to meditate, or a big change, like changing how you eat or moving to a new place and starting again, you've got to make a plan.

PART THREE

———— ◆ ————

Family

ELEVEN

WORKING MOTHER

Lead by example

◆

When Elon was born, I was twenty-three, the average age of a mother in 1971. It started with three days of false labor, which means contractions all day that disappear at night. The birth was hard, as he had a large head and was a big boy, eight pounds, eight ounces. I wanted a natural birth without painkillers; I can still feel the pain.

All the agony was forgotten when he arrived. I was so happy. He was this little cherub. I couldn't believe anything was so beautiful. He would lie next to me, and I would just stare at him.

It was the most wonderful thing that ever happened.

He was a hungry boy, and I was breastfeeding for three months. He would cry a lot, so at three months, I started supplementing with half-boiled milk, half-boiled water. By four months, he was pretty much on to full milk. By five months, he was eating baby cereals. Then pureed fruit, vegetables, and my normal meals. Elon loved to eat.

Pretty much the moment I stopped breastfeeding, I fell pregnant with Kimbal, who was born when I was twenty-four. Kimbal was a long, skinny guy, weighing a quarter pound more than his big brother. His was an easier birth. Again, I breastfed for three months, and when he was too hungry, I moved him on to milk and water, just as I had for Elon. I'd lectured to nurses that solids should start at six months, but my boys were big, so I started them earlier.

Once I wasn't breastfeeding, a few months later, I was pregnant again. I had my daughter when I was twenty-five. Tosca weighed a half pound less than Kimbal. It was a huge surprise and an absolute joy to have a daughter.

I carried my two younger kids under my arms, while my firstborn walked next to me. They were a handful, a wonderful handful.

With three births in three years and three weeks, the next time I went to the OB-GYN, he fitted me for an IUD, because my body needed to recover. He also could see my bruises.

By thirty-one, I was a single mother, and my priority was to take care of my children.

I was a working mother just as my parents were working parents. Unlike my parents, I did it by myself. My children are still the most important part of my life.

My mom never felt guilty about working full time. I never felt guilty about working full time, because I didn't have a choice. I worked to keep a roof over our heads, food in our

stomachs, and basic clothes on our backs. My children had to be responsible for themselves and be considerate of my work, as I had converted a bedroom into my office. There is no need to feel guilty. If you don't work, and you are resentful, it won't be fun for your kids. To have a better attitude, you'll need to make a plan to work either part time or full time and get help in whatever form you can. If you can arrange your work schedule so you can take your children and the neighbor's children to school, your neighbor can pick them up. You will need childcare for the afternoon until you come home, but you will come home happy and fulfilled. That's what I did.

When my children were young, I counseled my nutrition clients from home. When I modeled, there was a nanny for them. Sometimes they had to sit in the front row with their books while I did my runway shows.

My father always had his chiropractic practice next door, and my mom worked for him. My twin sister and I worked for him, too, from the age of eight. We were paid 5 cents an hour to help him mail out his monthly bulletin. We would have worked for free to help his business. My dad dictated the bulletin to my mom, who wrote it in shorthand, then typed it up.

It was our job to type the stencils and make the copies. Then Kaye and I would sit on the living room floor, fold the bulletin into three, put it in the envelope, and put the stamp on. We would do about one thousand of those every month. I was so young back then that I didn't even know there was such a thing as a marketing tool, but that's what it was. It taught me a lot for my own practice.

When Kaye and I were twelve, we started working in my dad's clinic as receptionists. From 6:45 to 7:30 in the morning, and from 4:00 to 6:00 in the afternoon, my twin sister and I took turns. We signed in the patients, made them tea, developed X-rays, and talked to them until my father was ready to see them.

We were treated like adults who could be trusted.

My parents' influence is evident in the lives my siblings and I chose and the way we raised our own children. My father was a scientist and ran a business, and I became a scientist and entrepreneur, and so did my brother Scott. My brother Lee had his own business school in South Africa, then served as a dean and vice-president academic at a large technical institution in Canada. My mother ran a dance school, and my sisters Kaye and Lynne ran dance schools.

From a young age, the kids helped me with my nutrition business. Tosca would go into my office and type up letters to doctors

on a word processor. She would add the doctor's name and address and basic greetings as well as the patient's name, and I would then fill it out with their consultation and possible outcomes. Elon was very good at helping to explain the word processor functions to me, not surprisingly! Kimbal was always helpful, too.

When we were living in Bloemfontein, I put Tosca to work at the modeling and image school I was running. She taught students how to walk, choreographed runway shows, and ran etiquette classes. She was a dresser for all my shows. She was around eight years old at the time.

What can I say? I needed help.

I brought my children up like my parents brought us up when we were young: to be independent, kind, honest, considerate, and polite, to work hard and do good things. I didn't treat them like babies or scold them. I never told them what to study. They just let me know what they were studying, or didn't. I didn't check their homework; that was their responsibility. It certainly hasn't hurt their careers. I think my siblings and I benefited, and my children benefited from taking responsibility early on.

As they got older, they continued to take responsibility for their own futures through the decisions they made. Tosca chose her own high school. They all applied to their universities of choice and completed their scholarship and student loan applications. I never even saw them.

Children don't need to be protected from the reality of responsibility. My kids benefited because they saw me work hard just to put a roof over our heads, put food in our stomachs, and purchase secondhand clothes. They want you to know how much I struggled, as life looks so easy for me now.

When they went to university, they lived in quite poor conditions, mattress on the floor, six housemates, or a dilapidated house, but they were fine with that.

If your children aren't used to luxuries, they survive well. You don't need to spoil them. Once you're sure your kids are in safe situations, let them look after themselves.

Being busy with my work did mean that they had freedom to get into antics sometimes, and I'm guessing I still know only some of the stories. (I like to think I was stern if they were irresponsible, but they would tell you I was a pushover.)

The kids remind me that when I was dating someone who was a smoker—and they didn't like him very much, as we were a very anti-smoking household—they put little firecrackers in his cigarettes. He lit one up, and it went BANG! They laughed and laughed. I thought it was quite funny, too. He didn't laugh. They never got punished for that.

It isn't that I didn't discipline them. I punished them if they were loud or naughty. They would have TV taken away from them or be sent to their room. Although now they tell me that when they were sent to their room, they would sneak back through the house and record their favorite TV shows on the old VHS and then run back to their rooms so that they didn't miss *The A-Team* or *MacGyver*. I would be in my office and would not notice that.

That's another benefit, they would say, to having a working mother.

TWELVE

THE MAGIC OF TWELVE

If children show interests, encourage them

◆

People ask me how I have raised such successful kids. I did it by letting them follow their interests.

I love my kids, and I'm so proud of them for everything that they have accomplished. My oldest child, Elon, is making electric cars to save the environment and launching rockets. My middle child, Kimbal, opened farm-to-table restaurants and is teaching children across the country to build fruit and vegetable gardens in underserved schools. My youngest child, Tosca, runs her own entertainment company, producing and directing romance films from bestselling novels. They all have different interests.

This reminds me of my siblings and me; we all went our own way. My parents were happy to support our different interests. In the same way, my children showed their interests at an early age, and to this day, they continue with the same interests and love them.

When they needed it, I encouraged them and helped them. When they wanted my advice, I gave it. I'm very short with my own answers, although I've tried to make them longer for this book. Ha-ha!

Kimbal said it quite nicely in an Instagram post. "My mother @MayeMusk has always been a guiding light in my life. In addition to being a CoverGirl at 70, she has two Master of Science degrees in nutrition and has always been passionate about #realfood. She is, and always has been, an inspiration to me. I'm so thankful for her support @BigGreen to educate the next generation about the power of planting, growing, and eating real food. Thank you, mom!!"

For my kids, they developed the interests that would become their careers by age twelve.

When Elon was young, I noticed that he read everything. I was a reader, too, but I would forget a story the moment it was done. Elon, on the other hand, remembered everything he read. He was always absorbing information. We called Elon the encyclopedia, because he had read the *Encyclopaedia Britannica* and *Colliers Encyclopedia*, and remembered everything. That's also why we called him Genius Boy. We could ask him anything. Remember, this was before the internet. I guess now we would call him The Internet.

He got his first computer at twelve. It was 1983, and computers were very, very new. He learned to use it and wrote a computer program, BLASTAR, which was a game. I showed it

to some university students who were in my modeling school. They were surprised that he knew all the coding shortcuts. These guys were in their second or third year in computer science, and they were very impressed.

I told him to submit it to a computer magazine.

He sent BLASTAR to *PC Magazine,* and they sent him 500 rand ($500). I don't think they knew he was twelve. It was published when he was thirteen. I didn't realize what he would go on to do.

When Kimbal was little, he always loved his food. It was when he was twelve that he took charge of mealtimes and started cooking for the family. He wanted food that tasted delicious, and if he had to do it himself to achieve that, he was willing. He loved to go to the grocery store with me. I remember going to

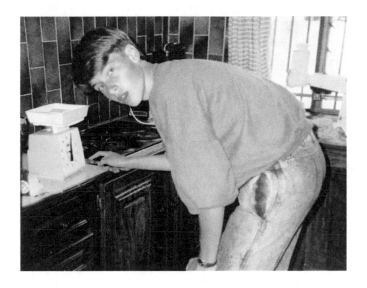

the market with him, and he would pick up a green pepper and smell it. And I would say, "Where do you come from?" I didn't find cooking a joy at all. I was feeding them healthy food, but it was quite simple: peanut butter sandwiches, peas, and carrots.

Kimbal would pick up all these new vegetables that we had never seen before, and he would cook with them. He would find a fresh fish that was caught that day and then cook it on the barbecue with tomatoes, lemons, and onions. He was a natural cook. He was great with vegetables, which were also very affordable, so that was perfect. Everything he made was delicious, and much better than my dull cooking.

When we moved to Toronto, he taught Elon how to prepare gnocchi Alfredo with crab so that he could cook for any girl-friends.

I felt very good when Kimbal told me recently that he felt

that I was always very supportive, no matter what he chose to do. He changed his career more than a few times! He studied business, became an internet entrepreneur, and then studied cooking at the French Culinary Institute in New York. I would go to his school dining room at 11:00 p.m. at the end of his shift to eat dinner with him. When he moved to Boulder and started a restaurant called the Kitchen in a former restaurant space, I scrubbed the stoves and fridges to make them shine. Unfortunately, they were replaced! Oh well . . .

Kimbal has had quite a journey. After an accident while he was tubing with his kids, a broken neck left him with a lot of time to think about what he really wanted to be doing with his life. Restaurants were his passion, so he wound up opening farm-to-table restaurants in middle America and starting the nonprofit Big Green. These are learning gardens in under-served schools. He also started a company called Square Roots, teaching young entrepreneurs to be urban farmers, building gardens in recycled shipping containers in parking lots.

Looking back at what he loved at twelve, it makes perfect sense.

When Tosca was twelve and in grade seven, her drama teacher decided not to run the drama club anymore. So Tosca took over.

My daughter was always very much an actress. She was into theater, dance, performing, and music at a very young age, and she always loved movies.

In Johannesburg, we would spend Friday nights on the couch together, watching romance movies and eating ice cream (when I was not watching what I ate the way I do now). She was always

in every performing arts club. So of course it makes sense to me now that she's a director, making her own films, turning romance novels into movies for her company, Passionflix.

I'm always thrilled to get dressed up and join her on the red carpet for her premieres.

Parents are really stressed about their kids. I saw that in my nutrition practice. A father or mother would be stress eating because there were so many forms to fill out to get their kids into a good school or university. I would tell them to let their kids complete their own documents to get themselves into universities or jobs. They should be responsible for their future. If they prefer to start a business and you think it's a good idea, support them. Teach your children good manners. But let them decide what they want.

I could not have predicted Tesla or SpaceX or the Kitchen or Big Green or Passionflix. But now I see that what Elon is accomplishing with technology, what Kimbal is building in the world of food, and what Tosca is doing with movies: all of it is rooted in what they loved as kids.

THIRTEEN

STARTING OVER

Say yes to make your life more interesting

◆

S tarting over is hard, especially if it means moving to a new place.

In the eight cities I moved to as an adult, my first year was lonely, my second year I made a few friends, but by my third year, I had many friends I really enjoyed. I just had to accept the fact that starting over is hard. The main reason is, I work on my own. I wasn't in an office where I could connect with colleagues. That's also why I started by contacting all the dietitians to get together. Some became friends. Some are still friends.

When you start again somewhere new, you have to get out. You can't sit and wallow in your loneliness and hope your social life and business pick up. You have to get out and socialize and network with people. You have to start meeting people, because that's where your work comes from. That's where your friends and partners come from. You know, you have to kiss a lot of frogs before one turns into a prince. In a new place, even getting out to try to socialize feels like work. That's because it is.

It's not easy being on your own at events. It's stressful. Nobody knows you, and everybody's air-kissing and hugging each other. All you can do is stand there. You can't interfere in their friendship circles and their little crowds; that would be weird. If you're lucky, someone will be nice enough to come over and say hi to you. I sometimes give myself one hour to have someone talk to me, then I will leave. I have seldom left a party.

I learned that when I was thirty-one and newly divorced. A friend said to me, "Go out all the time. It's the only way you can start meeting people in a new town." I did, but I felt often as though I was sticking out like a sore thumb.

I have since realized that everyone has this feeling, too. Sometimes even celebrities can be alone. When I was running the modeling school in Bloemfontein, I was asked to take my students to the airport to welcome Miss Universe. She stood there alone. I was very polite and didn't want to approach her and impose.

It was exactly what I had experienced at parties when I didn't know anybody, until somebody took pity on me. I thought, "I remember that feeling."

I went over and said, "Hello. I'm the director of the modeling school. I just wanted to welcome you."

She said, "Thank you for talking to me! It's horrible to stand alone!"

So remember: even Miss Universe feels awkward at parties.

. . .

With my completed master's degree in hand, I moved from Bloemfontein back to Johannesburg to be closer to my family. I had to build up my practice quickly.

If you go to a job where you are surrounded by the same people every day at your work, they can become your friends. I didn't network to build my career; I networked with my colleagues to learn more about what is going on and to share my success as a dietitian in private practice. I wanted more dietitians to be available to open their own practice and to dispel all the fad diets that are so popular. However, it did end up that my colleagues were good to me and referred me for talks, spokesperson work, and media work and sent me counseling clients. Connecting with people will increase your business more than sitting alone waiting for the phone to ring. And, nowadays, waiting for emails to arrive.

My strategy, along with accepting invitations, was to join every association that I could. I joined the Dietetics Association and got a list of dietitians in my area. If you can get on some committees, that's where you are seeing the same people and can get to know them. I started holding a meeting for dietitians who were in private practice or wanted to be, gave some advice on how to be successful, and then we all had time to chat. I got to meet new people, and they met each other. My colleagues appreciated it so much that I decided to keep doing it.

Over that time, I was building up a solid list of clients. After two years, I was seeing twenty clients a day!

. . .

Then the unthinkable happened: my phone stopped working. The phone cable to my home office was damaged, and as this was in the eighties, South Africa was not manufacturing such things. It was going to take six months for the cable to come from Europe.

The phone was how I made all my appointments and the only way my clients could reach me unless they stopped by or wrote a letter. To make matters worse, there was no message letting people know that my number was out of service. If they tried to ring me, all they would get was a busy signal! I needed a plan if I was going to survive. I thought I had it figured out, so I bought a pager and sent letters to all my clients and doctors, letting them know that all they had to do was page me, and I would find a phone and return their calls.

That plan didn't work. Within three weeks, I had only one client each day.

I was falling apart. I was losing income steadily. I didn't know what I would do.

At the next meeting with my colleagues that I had organized, they told me they had been trying to call me, but my phone was always busy. I broke down and cried. Then something wonderful happened. They told me I'd been helping them for two years; now it was their time to help me. They passed on six of their part-time consultancy jobs to me— nursing home, private clinic, research on infant feeding, writing, teaching, and giving nutrition advice at a supermarket. Each job required four to eight hours a week and no phone calls. I was excited to be working again and exploring a new area of nutrition that I hadn't done before.

When the phone cable was repaired, my practice picked up again, and I was busier than ever! And consulting became a new form of income, which would help me for the rest of my nutrition career. Sometimes the best plan is accepting help.

This also worked well when one of my fellow dietitians stepped forward with information about a job for one of my kids.

When we were newly moved to Toronto, Elon needed to find work. I attended a dietitians meeting, and I mentioned that my son needed a job. One of the dieticians' husbands worked at Microsoft.

"My son is great with computers," I told her. Every mother says things like that. In this case, they were very surprised to find out how right I was.

Throughout my career, I have always worked hard to help others be successful. The surprising part was that sometimes I needed their support as well. Don't be good to others just to get something in return; do it because you enjoy it, and it helps them do better.

At seventy-one, I have met some of my best friends through my work over the years. And I continue to make so many wonderful friends in my nutrition and modeling careers!

Now, when I go to any event and I see someone standing alone, I walk up to them and include them in our conversation. If you see someone else who is completely alone, talk to him or her, too. You could embarrass yourself, but actually you don't. Mostly, you meet nice people that way.

FOURTEEN

CHANGE COUNTRIES, IF NECESSARY

Take a chance; you can always return

◆

L ife is unpredictable and full of surprises. Sometimes you just need to take a chance and make a big change.

I was forty-one, my business was going well in Johannesburg, and we had a nice house. Finally, I felt secure.

Elon wanted to move to Canada. He felt like North America was the right place to pursue his computer interests. He asked me to apply to regain my citizenship so the three kids could all get citizenship.

Tosca wanted to join him because she thought it would be more fun. When Tosca was thirteen, she had wanted to study French at the Alliance Française, just in case she moved to Canada. She became very interested in her French lessons, because she had read that French was the second language of Canada.

I took lessons as well. I had studied French at school, so I was in the advanced class. Each class at Alliance Française was holding a performance, and my class said, "We need an opera singer." None of us were talented.

I said, "My daughter can do it!"

They said, "But she's in the beginner's class. She can't speak French."

I said, "We'll figure it out."

We rented a gold opera gown and wig, and she performed in French. Even though she was so young, even though she didn't speak French, she took on this challenge and gave a great performance.

No one recognized her! Some remarked that it was unfair that we'd brought in a singer. They were shocked to find out it was Tosca, who was just thirteen.

She was still panicked about not being an expert in French, because in South Africa, if you didn't pass your Afrikaans exams, you failed your grade. She was convinced that we were going to move and thought that if she arrived in Canada and didn't know how to speak French, she would fail her subjects.

It took a long time to get it all sorted. When the passports finally arrived, Elon was on his way to Canada three weeks later. He was seventeen.

I sent him with addresses and $2,000 in traveler's checks. The money was from the original 100 rand I had won in my first beauty competition twenty years before. A friend told me to put my winnings into stocks. When the bottom of the market fell out in 1969 and the R100 dropped to R10, I opened an account in Elon's name after he was born and forgot about it. In 1989, I found that account, and it was worth $2,000. Now he had some money to survive on for a few weeks.

I wrote to my family in Canada to let them know that he was coming, although of course he got to them before the letters did. At that time, letters took six weeks to get there.

He landed in Montreal and called my uncle, but there was no answer. He called me collect and said, "What do I do now?"

I told him to find a YMCA. Then he traveled to Toronto to find another uncle, who wasn't there either. So he took a bus to Saskatchewan to find my cousins.

He just turned up on their doorstep and said, "Hi, I'm Maye's son." That is where he turned eighteen.

Tosca, who was going on fifteen by then, said to me, "Maybe we should join Elon. Go and see what he is doing."

But I had been accepted to the University of Cape Town for my PhD.

I said, "I'll do my degree here, and we can go after that."

She said, "If we don't move, I'll go to Canada, and Elon will look after me."

I thought that was nonsense, but I agreed to go and see what was going on. I had no interest in moving, but Elon was already there. Kimbal said he wanted to go when he finished high school, and Tosca was so determined, I certainly wasn't going to let them go by themselves. At the very least, I could go and check it out.

I found two dietitians who agreed to take over my practice while I traveled. They stayed in my home to look after Tosca.

When I went to Canada to see about opportunities, Elon and I traveled together to universities in five provinces. Each university was willing to take me on except for Montreal, because they said my French wasn't good enough to do research work.

I became interested in the University of Toronto, because they would pay me as a research officer to work ten hours per week so I could also run my practice, study, and model. Toronto was also the center for modeling in Canada. And as I was a staff member, my children would be able to study for free.

I went to all the modeling agencies in five major cities. I was in my early forties, so I wasn't sure about the reception I'd receive. But they each said yes, they could use an older model.

I came back to Johannesburg three weeks later and found that Tosca had sold my home, my furniture, and my car. This five-foot-ten fifteen-year-old who did not care that she was young and had no permission just sold it all. Everything in the house was gone. And my car.

All I had to do was sign the papers, and it was done. We left the country a few weeks after that. The plan was that Kimbal would finish his studies and then join us.

Many people have asked why I wasn't mad at Tosca for selling my home, car, and furniture. Well, she had a point. We had discussed moving to Canada eventually; she just wanted to speed up the process. If a family member makes a good point, even if it's a drastic change, go with it.

Moving to Toronto was good for our family because there were new opportunities. I was at my peak in Johannesburg and happy to be there, but my children saw a future in America. We could start in Canada. We knew it would be hard in the beginning, but when we proved ourselves, it helped in the long-term.

In the short-term, the surprise was that I would never fear my ex-husband again, after twenty years of hell. To live without fear is wonderful. Even if you don't know if moving will be good for you and your family, you can always go back. I never went back.

If it's time to move ahead, take a chance, give it three years, try really hard to get settled. If your life hasn't improved and you are very unhappy, go back to your former situation.

FIFTEEN

ACTS OF KINDNESS

Appreciate good deeds

◆

You worry about many things that never happen, yet horrible things can happen to you that you didn't foresee. Don't try to figure these out. You can plan and you can prepare, but you can never be sure in advance what is going to happen. Tosca had been so worried about being held back by language, so we had gone and studied French in preparation, but when we moved to Toronto, we found out that nobody in that city spoke French.

But still plenty of other things went wrong. We did our best. Many people were kind to us. Some were friends, and some were just good strangers.

Just before we left South Africa, a friend told us of someone in Toronto who could rent us a furnished apartment for the first few months that I could pay for in South Africa, the first of many helping hands. This was useful because the South African government would block my funds after I left and would not allow me to take out anything other than $2,000, and I needed to pay my rent right away.

Tosca and I moved to Toronto and into an apartment. There was one bedroom, and Tosca and I slept in the bed in the bedroom, and Elon slept on the couch in the living room. We arrived in December, which is bitterly cold in Toronto. Our clothes were like Miami clothes, not quite suitable for that freezing-cold weather. We must have borrowed coats from my sister and mother, which were either twenty or fifty years old.

We had a lot to learn. I didn't know the city well, and it was terribly confusing to make my way around. I couldn't afford a car, so I was always on the subways and buses. All I knew was that you had to use a loonie, which is a heavy one-dollar coin, to take the subway and the buses.

For the first couple of weeks, I carried a huge bag of one-dollar coins to pay for the bus, then pay for the subway, then pay for the bus, because I had to go to so many different places for auditions and while looking for a rental apartment.

One day, I was on the bus and there were some tourists who asked the bus driver for a transfer. They took the transfer and went to the subway. I said, "There's a transfer?"

It was a fabulous thing to learn. I had lined up some modeling jobs, but in order to get to them, I had to travel quite a distance. Now I could use a transfer to go in one direction everywhere. It was such a relief not to carry those heavy bags of coins, and also a financial relief.

. . .

At forty-two, I was eager to start my practice in Toronto, but I couldn't begin until I was a registered dietitian (RD), which meant I needed to pass the Canadian exams. Simultaneously, I needed to take five undergrad exams from the University of Toronto to show that my grades qualified me for graduate work. For registration, I had to take the same exams as newly graduated dietetic students who were in their early twenties. Fortunately, for the first time, I got to study in English, which was fantastic!

On the day of the exam, I had a TV commercial that I desperately needed to do due to my financial circumstances. In an incredible act of kindness, one of the staff dietitians at the nutritional sciences department agreed to oversee my exam on another afternoon.

At a dietitians meeting, a colleague said that she was unable to teach childhood nutrition education at a college two nights a week, and she offered that position to me. The college was willing to acknowledge my Master of Science degree from South Africa and didn't need me to be a registered dietitian. Suddenly, I had another job.

In the meantime, I was modeling. I could always tell who was a model, because they were tall and thin and were all carrying a huge bag. We did our own hair and makeup, and we always carried our own shoes, accessories, wigs, and hair pieces. It wasn't like I was doing couture shows.

I had a lot of modeling experience, but I only had experience with how things were done in South Africa.

At the first rehearsal I went to in Toronto, I was the mother of the bride.

The producer said, "Why are you wearing sandals? You need fall hose and pumps."

I didn't know what she was saying.

I said, "I'm not a fireman. What are hose? What are pumps?"

Of course, hose are stockings, and pumps are high-heeled shoes. How would I know that? Those are the kinds of things you learn when you move to new countries.

She called my agency to complain. I was nearly in tears because I needed to work and I was being treated badly for being unprofessional. One of the models overheard the complaint and said to me, "There's a store in Toronto with shoes for $19."

I bought a pair of silver shoes and a pair of gold shoes, and I wore them for every runway show until my financial status improved. An act of kindness, by a model.

It was the middle of winter, and on my flight to Toronto, my luggage had gone missing with all my clothes and my degrees. Of course the bag full of Tosca's stuffed toys arrived unharmed.

Until I had my luggage, I was stuck wearing Elon's and Tosca's clothes, because I couldn't afford to buy new clothes. I had to explain to people why I was dressed in such a strange fashion.

I kept on saying, "Sorry, my bags are missing."

Every month I would rent a car and go to the airline at the airport and ask them about my luggage. Every month they would say, "Sorry, we don't know where it is."

A few months later, I explained my strange outfit to a man I had met in Toronto.

He said, "What do you mean, they can't find your luggage? I'm taking you to the airport." He picked me up, which was so great, because I didn't have to pay for a car rental. He had no idea how poor I was.

We go to the airline's office, and he walked in and said, "I'm her lawyer. You will find her luggage."

They said, "Yes, sir."

He was an accountant. I laughed so hard. I couldn't believe it.

The next day, they called him and said, "We found the bags in Mexico City." Three days later, I had my two huge bags. One was slightly damaged. One sweater was missing. But my degrees were there!

A wonderful act of kindness, from a man who was not a lawyer.

I had booked a modeling job in Mississauga, a forty-minute drive from Toronto—if you had a car. When I woke up, I found that it was snowing. Well, if you have to get to work, you find a way to get there, even in blizzards. I packed my shoes in my big bag and set off. I had to take two buses, two subway trains, two more buses, and then walk about four hundred yards to get to the studio, in three feet of snow.

I couldn't see the sidewalks. There was a lamppost, and there was a road for the cars, and I just assumed the sidewalk was between them, but I couldn't see anything. I was the sole walker, trudging through three feet of snow to get to this studio. It had taken me two hours to get there.

When I checked in, they said, "Thank you for driving in this terrible weather."

I said, "No, I took the bus." They were dumbstruck.

We did the shoot, and afterward, I traipsed through that thick snow back to the road.

Far ahead, at the end of the road, I saw a bus stopped. I kept walking, and as I passed, the driver opened the door.

I asked, "Are you stuck?"

He said, "No, I saw you walking, so I waited for you. You could only have been walking to catch a bus, because there was nowhere else to walk to."

I was the only one in the bus. A wonderful act of kindness, by a bus driver.

My lesson here is that appreciating kindness from strangers will make you feel happy. I didn't realize how many people had been kind to me until I wrote this book. Then you remember. Life was made easier because people were nice. They would help me out of uncomfortable, unhappy, or difficult situations. They didn't expect anything in return. Those are good people, and there are many. Appreciate the good things that are happening in your life. When you are in a tough situation, look for support from family, friends, and even strangers. And be kind to strangers, too.

PART FOUR

———— ♦ ————

Success

SIXTEEN

WOMAN AT WORK

The harder you work, the luckier you get

◆

My father's motto was "The harder you work, the luckier you get." People would say to my dad how lucky he was to be successful. People say the same to me, but they are wrong. My family and friends have seen how hard I've worked and my struggles, and they wanted me to share them in my book. None of them has said I'm lucky. It may look like a huge stroke of luck to be on a billboard in Times Square or to be a Cover-Girl at sixty-nine. And it is! But you have to work hard to make your own luck.

We were only able to take a little bit of money with us when we moved to Toronto. I had worked so hard and finally become comfortable in Johannesburg, but because my funds were blocked, I had to start over.

My accountant was able to send a small amount monthly for each student, and with four of us studying, that gave us a small sum to cover our groceries. I was working as a researcher for ten hours a week, and that covered our rent-controlled apartment. I started modeling right away, and that covered everything else.

I had started working at the university immediately and was so busy that I didn't have time to figure out schools for Tosca.

She gathered a whole bunch of pamphlets on her own so that she could choose a school in the neighborhood. That took care of school. But when she got home, she realized that she had nothing to do in the condo complex we were staying in. So she went to a nearby hamburger place and asked for a job.

They said, "How many days do you want to work?"

She said, "Oh, I'll work every day."

They said, "You may legally work only six days per week."

They then asked how many hours she wanted to work. She said twelve hours per day. They said she may legally work only eight hours per day. She was learning about the law and for the first time working for someone else.

She started right away to work at that place all day, then, when school started, after school.

At the hamburger joint, she was mopping floors, taking out garbage, and cleaning toilets, which she had never done before. It was a very different world from what she was used to in South Africa, where she had a bedroom that was designed to her specifications, with a closet that took up the entire wall. She had the best room in the house.

Now she was sharing a bedroom with me and cleaning bathrooms at a fast food outlet.

But she saw it as an adventure. She said to herself, "This is the job," and she did it. She never complained.

She ate burgers and French fries all month. That was an experience in itself because in South Africa, she did not have fast food. She worked as a cleaner for only a month, then was promoted to the assistant manager of the drive-thru.

Eventually Tosca found a new job that was closer to our home. This time, it was at a high-end supermarket, and her salary nearly doubled. This was a lesson in economics for her, and she's never forgotten it.

She's a brilliant negotiator now. And she's fair to everyone who works for her. She appreciates people with a work ethic and who work long hours.

It wasn't easy in Toronto, but we were learning quickly. I was working as a model, but I couldn't get a credit card because I had no credit rating. Every application was denied. That meant that we were stuck living on whatever cash was on hand. Whenever I got a paycheck from a modeling job, it meant that we could afford something else, like warmer coats and shoes or linens and blankets for our home.

No matter how many banks I approached, I couldn't get a card because I had no credit; without a credit card, I couldn't begin to build my credit history in the country. If I didn't build credit, it would be impossible to get a rental lease for a car, an office, anything. None of the banks would give me a break.

Somebody told me that the department stores would be more lenient and sent me off to apply for a store card so that I could begin to build my credit.

I went to Eaton's, which was a large and sophisticated department store.

They said no.

They explained that there was no way to be sure that I could make good on the payments. But on the wall of the office over the desk was a Mother's Day poster, and I was the model. I pointed it out to them.

They were delighted. They said, "We'll give you a card."

That was a lucky break. Then I remembered the shoot for Eaton's: I had taken the day off from university and ridden the subway and the bus to get to the studio. It was really worth it.

I was born into privilege. I had good parents who gave me a sound education. With continued education at my expense, I managed to build up my business in eight cities in three countries. With regard to modeling, I look like my pretty mom and got my height from my handsome dad, so I was lucky. Modeling gave me that little extra income. And now, at seventy-one, a really good income. I could call that luck, except that I worked hard at modeling for fifty years, and still work hard to maintain my health and my weight—every minute, every hour, of every day. That isn't luck. That is really hard work.

If you aren't born into privilege, you need to find your talent and work hard at it. Share it with the world through social media and everyone around you. I would say you have to forget how you were born. There is a saying: "At twenty-one you are no longer an orphan." This means, you need to take responsibility for your future life. The harder you work, the easier it is for luck to find you.

SEVENTEEN

ASK FOR WHAT YOU WANT

Persistence leads to success

◆

W hen the kids were young, I always taught them to ask for what they wanted.

Tosca was eleven when I took her to see the American singer Laura Branigan's concert. She was a big fan. I knew the photographer of the resort where the concert was. He gave us tickets, because we couldn't afford them. He also gave Tosca a picture of Laura onstage, singing.

The next day, we were sitting at a table in a restaurant, and nearby, incredibly, was Laura Branigan herself, having lunch.

Tosca wanted to get her autograph, but she was terrified. She kept saying, "I can't go and ask her for an autograph."

I said, "Well, if you don't ask her, it's already no. But if you do ask her, there's a chance she'll say yes. So your answer is either a no, or maybe a yes."

Tosca thought about it and said, "Okay."

She went over and asked.

At first Laura said, "Wait! How did you get this photo?" She had never seen it. Tosca told her from the resort's photographer. So Laura signed it. Tosca beamed. This was a huge success. She has never forgotten that.

When Tosca was looking for investors for Passionflix, Kimbal said, "If they keep on meeting you, it means they are still interested." And she has found that to be true.

If they say definitely no, you move on.

But if they don't say no, you have to keep trying until you get to that one yes.

Every time I moved to a new city, I had to build up my nutrition practice again. In South Africa, it was easier—doctors were always thrilled that I was opening an office near their practice and would send me patients right away, so I expected even more enthusiasm in Canada. But that isn't the way it happened.

If I wanted patients, I was going to have to ask for what I wanted. I started by writing letters to the doctors in Toronto to tell them that I could help their patients. I discovered that most of these letters were ignored, as they go to the office manager. Still, you can usually expect a few responses if you mail out one hundred notices.

After I sent out the first group of letters in Toronto, I thought my phone was out of order, because *nobody* was calling me. I started calling the doctors' offices. Most office managers would say that the doctors didn't want to see me. If I kept calling others, I felt sure I could get to twenty who would agree to set up an appointment. And I did. I was following my own advice: there's no such thing as a guaranteed yes, but if you don't ask, it's a guaranteed no.

I'd sit in the waiting room, sometimes for an hour, waiting for my appointment. I'd ask the doctors to send their patients to me who had pre-diabetes, high cholesterol, or high blood pressure. I knew if I could get them to improve their eating habits, their blood values would improve within three months. An added benefit was avoiding the side effects of drugs.

Doctors were reluctant to send patients to me. They would say, "Insurance doesn't cover nutrition counseling; they cover drugs for weight loss."

Or they would say, "Patients won't listen to you."

I knew that patients would listen, if I just had a chance. If they would send a few patients, I would show them results. When you have good eating habits, you have more energy and feel fantastic, but it takes time and persistence. That was the basis of my nutrition counseling. Eventually, four doctors sent me a few patients as a trial run.

Real results don't happen overnight. A patient might come with labs stating high blood sugar. Three months later, if they would stick to their meal plan, they would lose twenty pounds. Their blood sugar levels would be normal, and their risk for diabetes would decrease.

Once the patients' results showed marked improvement and the doctors took notice, I started to become very busy. It took around six months before I was seeing clients from 7:30 a.m. to 7:30 p.m. On weekends and holidays, I did my paperwork and sent out patient reports and more letters of introduction with brochures describing my work. I started approaching newspapers, magazines, and TV stations for media work. That was not easy. They were not interested. I was still an unknown.

In an effort to become more known, I attended dietitian conferences while developing talks so that I could get more speaking engagements. Again, a long process. I did one talk on nutrition, and then I sent the brochures out to corporations. I did another talk, and then I sent out more brochures. Eventually I was giving many talks and was consulting to the food industry. I soon became chair of the Consulting Dietitians of Ontario, then president of the Consulting Dietitians of Canada. Now the media would call *me* all the time, asking me to comment on stories in the news or with questions about nutrition.

In 1994, four years after we arrived in Toronto, I gave a talk for the Canadian Dietetic Association. There was a publishing executive in the audience.

After my talk, she said to me, "I want you to a write a book!"

This happened only because I persisted.

Some women can be shy, or lacking in confidence, or scared of rejection, so they don't want to ask for what they want. Men don't seem to have that problem. They think they're fabulous and deserve a better job, a raise, more benefits, the corner office with windows, even if they're obnoxious and incompetent. We've seen that way too often.

I remember meeting someone who had just been fired. I asked her where she was going to find another job. She said she had put it out to the universe to provide. I said sending out a résumé could be better. If you send out twenty résumés and don't get a job, welcome to my world.

Remember that persistence works, sometimes. Not all the time—if you ask and they say no, you move on. But if you want something, you've got to keep asking.

EIGHTEEN

FEEL FANTASTIC

Don't wallow in disappointments

◆

All my children had gone off to universities, which was 100 percent their choice. I was at the University of Toronto, and my children could have studied there for free if they chose medicine or law. They would have stayed with me with no rental or food expenses. They preferred to go it on their own. Elon chose physics and business, Kimbal studied business, and Tosca studied film. They had to get their own grants and loans and support themselves, and they all did. I was happy that they chose to be independent and go their own way. Maybe they were tired of my bean soup.

People said that I was going to suffer from empty-nest syndrome, because I lived for my kids. That made sense, as many of my clients would be sad when their children left home, so I thought it was going to happen to me. But it didn't! I loved it. It seems that other people's problems are not necessarily your own. I remember this saying by a ninety-year-old: "Ninety-five percent of the things you worry about never happen."

By the time Tosca left, I said, "I can't believe my freedom."

I was living on my own for the very first time in twenty years. I could now exercise at night, not care about food at home, and walk around naked! After trying that once, I preferred a T-shirt. Until I got my book deal . . . then I was writing for about five hours at night, and twelve hours on the weekends. It took me three months to write my first draft.

I couldn't wait to share it with my kids.

Once a month, I would visit one of my children. I would save $2,000 a month, and that $2,000 would have to cover my flight and anything they needed. I would find the cheapest flights and would take a bus to the airport because I couldn't afford the shuttle. Sometimes I could get a flight for $150. The rest of the money was spent on them, for whatever they wanted, whether it was food, clothes, or furniture.

I was going to Wharton to see Elon. I said, "What do you want to do?"

Elon said, "Let's go to New York."

We took a train to New York, walked around, did the touristy thing. We were sitting at Rockefeller Center, and I gave him my manuscript to read. It was all about calories, metabolism, essential nutrients—fascinating information.

Elon started reading it, and he said, "This is boring."

I said, "What do you mean?"

He said, "Why are you seeing twenty-five clients a day? What do they want to know?"

I said, "Well, they're coming to me for nutrition advice."

"Then that's what you put in the book," he said.

Even at that age, he showed his wisdom. So I listened to him. From then on, every time a client came to see me, I would tell them that I was writing a book and ask if I could take notes at our sessions, but I wouldn't mention them by name.

They were full of advice for the book! Besides meal plans, they wanted me to talk about image and self-esteem, because I would tell them to change their hair, their clothes, stand up straight, and smile when they came to see me.

I wrote about all that in my book. The next time I showed it to my children, the responses were a little more enthusiastic. I had help from everyone. Kimbal edited my first book five times. Tosca said she did it six times. I remember my mom reading the book out loud to see how it flowed. I was fortunate to have a family who helped each other become successful.

When the publishers received it, they called it *Feel Fantastic,* because that's how they felt when they read it. They also said that they wanted me on the cover. They paid for my photo shoot, and I used a photographer I knew, and Julia did my styling. I wore a red slack suit, which was the most expensive suit I'd ever bought. However, I got my money's worth, because I wore it over and over at my talks. In those days, there wasn't social media, so no one realized I was wearing the same suit at every talk.

Finally, my career felt like it was coming together. My speaking bookings were increasing, which also helped to sell the book. One of my speaking engagements was at Kellogg's headquarters. I included eating well and self-esteem, because it does make you feel better and more confident when you have more energy and are eating nutritious foods. This led to a huge breakthrough, when Kellogg's approached my publisher to put my book cover on a box of Special K cereals, as part of their campaign to promote women's self-esteem.

I was the first dietitian whose book was on a cereal box, with me on the cover! That really made me feel fantastic! Kaye was thrilled to go to the supermarket and see my cereal box taking up a whole shelf space.

She told a stranger walking by, "That's my twin!"

Instead of being impressed, he fled.

When Kaye told me this, we laughed and laughed.

. . .

At this point I was feeling very confident about my practice, my kids studying, and my book. I had been renting for so long, and at forty-six, I felt ready to take on a new challenge: home ownership. It was time.

I had saved up some money, and there was a beautiful little two-story house for sale that was next to my office in Toronto. In Canada at that time, you only had to have a 5 percent deposit. The house was $200,000, and I had $10,000 in the bank. This was the first time I had ever had savings.

I went to the bank and completed my application at the high-end shopping mall. I thought it might help that the manager had seen me modeling there. They knew I was working. I was sure they would accept my application. After two weeks went by and I didn't hear from them, I went in and said, "By the way, you were going to contact me a week ago regarding my application."

The manager was embarrassed and said, "You were rejected."

They said my income hadn't been high enough over the past five years, I was the sole owner of my practice, which made me a high risk for a mortgage.

I was surprised and deflated. I had been an excellent client, and they had seen me modeling in their shopping mall. And now I was rejected. However, I had to get back to my practice, and I didn't have time to wallow in my disappointments. This just meant that my plan was delayed, and I would have to save more to prove myself.

. . .

While this was going on, Kimbal was working in Toronto and using my office phone to talk to Elon every day. After the phone bill came in at $800, I told him that he should go and join Elon in Palo Alto, California. So he moved to Silicon Valley to try to launch their first technology company at the start of the internet boom. Their first company was called Zip2, which offered maps and door-to-door directions, and they worked with the world's major newspapers to bring them online. These were entirely new ideas, and I thought they were good ones that would make life better. I wanted to do anything I could to support them. I was visiting them every six weeks as they were getting their business plan going. I bought them food, clothing, and furniture and covered their printing expenses. They couldn't get a credit card in the US, so they were using my Canadian credit card.

Nearly out of money, they needed some cash to continue. Fortunately, I still had $10,000 in the bank. I gave it to them because I believed in what they were doing.

The night before they had meetings with venture capitalists, Kimbal and I went to Kinko's to print out their presentations in color. I was paying for it because it was a dollar a page, and that was very expensive.

The next morning, we were all exhausted because none of us had slept. Of course, Elon was fine, because he never sleeps. He was always up late doing the coding for their program.

They had been seeing numerous VCs and pitching their idea for months. That morning they met two VCs who made them their first offer. We were delirious with happiness.

That night I said, "We're going to the best restaurant in town."

We went to a fabulous restaurant, and we all looked worn-out and grubby. But they treated us wonderfully. We don't know why they were so nice. I don't even know what we ate. We'd been eating Jack in the Box and that type of thing—anything quick, inexpensive, and open at two in the morning. Kimbal told me he can still taste their chicken fajita pita.

The bill came. I paid it and said, "That's the last time you'll see my credit card."

And it was.

To sum things up, I learned that you should never wallow in disappointment. If you are disappointed, go in a different direction. If you were dumped or didn't get that job, forget about it and keep going. If you're rejected for a home mortgage, keep working to improve your credit rating. All that has happened to me over and over. I haven't been successful in marriage and relationships. I've been rejected from numerous jobs over and over. My life has derailed to such an extent that I actually moved cities and countries.

In relationships, I would be dumped by a guy and be sad for six months, then three months, then three weeks, then three days. I wish I hadn't wallowed so much in the beginning. Wallowing makes you unattractive and annoying and will keep people away from you. When my nutrition clients would come in with a sad face, I would tell them to walk upright and smile. I wouldn't allow them to make my day miserable. They would laugh, and thank me for that advice. When I desperately needed extra income from modeling and would be rejected from a job that I thought I nearly had, it would make me scared. Now I'm used to it. And will even say that now I have extra time for my dog. He's always happy when I'm around. The great thing about aging is that when you have a disappointment, you've already been through that. You recover much quicker.

My advice to you is to stay as positive as you can. Time heals. Try to recover from disappointment quicker than I did. And maybe get a dog.

NINETEEN

MOVE AHEAD

Starting over could be the best thing you do

♦

Everyone has reasons for moving from one place to another. There has to be a really good reason to move, as moving is hard.

My mother moved from Moose Jaw to Regina to start her business, and in between, she got her dance education in big cities like New York and Chicago. My father left the farm he grew up on to become a chiropractor and moved to Regina where he met my mom. When we moved to South Africa, he chose Pretoria for the beautiful lilac jacaranda trees.

The first moves I did were for my education or career. Later, because I felt I had to or to get away from bad situations. And later still, to be near my children or find the places where I would be happy. Also, I get very restless and like to explore and learn about new cities, new countries, new cultures. My twin sister says I have ants in my pants. And when my children moved, they did so for opportunity, for education, and to build their own families. I moved to be close to them, far from them, and then close to them again.

As an adult, I have lived in three countries and nine cities. It's always hard to move. And it's particularly a huge deal to move to new countries. When the Canadian law changed and I could pass citizenship on to my children when they wanted to move to North America, it took months of paperwork, lining up to discuss paperwork, sitting in a waiting room requesting advice, submitting pages and pages of documents, then more documents. When I eventually received my Canadian citizenship, I was told I didn't need all those documents as I had been born in Canada.

In Toronto, I moved twice; in New York, I moved three times. I plan way ahead, packing only things that are worth the cost of moving. I used to pack many research journals, which took up a lot of room and were very heavy and expensive to move. Fortunately, now with the internet, I just have to pack a laptop. All the research work is online. You have to be very organized. But you do get rid of a lot of garbage—physically and mentally!

Although I was happy and successful in Toronto, my children wanted me to live closer to them. I hadn't been thinking about moving at all. I thought that I would live in Toronto forever. That had been my plan. Perhaps it was time for a new plan.

To move to the USA was even harder than previous moves. My father had been born in Minneapolis, so I went to the U.S. Consulate General in Toronto to see if this was possible. I waited with two hundred other potential emigrants for hours. Then they gave me many documents to complete and I had to find proof of my documents. It took six months of going to the consulate general and waiting for half a day to find out I couldn't get US citizenship as my father had moved to Canada more than six years before I was born. So, that door was closed. I then had to apply for an H1B visa. This took months.

At forty-eight, I had to study on my own to pass the American exams and practice nutrition in the US. This meant I had to learn a lot more biochemistry, but I had to do it in imperial measurements: ounces and pounds, feet and inches, instead of the metric system, which is used in the rest of the world. You can't believe how hard it is to learn both systems, but it helps when I speak internationally.

I had terrible sciatica at the time, so I couldn't socialize. But I could work, very painfully, and lie on my back and study. That's a bonus, if you can see it that way. Surprisingly, I passed the exams, sold my Toronto practice, and moved in with my sons in Mountain View.

But when I got there, there was no mountain and no view. And no kids, because they worked day and night. Kimbal doesn't even remember that I stayed with him and Elon for three weeks, and rightly so, because they were always working.

I said, "I need a life. I need to move to a bigger city. I need to move to San Francisco."

. . .

My budget was very tight, because I had yet to start a practice, and the money I had made from selling my last practice wasn't going to last for very long.

I borrowed Kimbal's car and drove to San Francisco to find an apartment. Because I didn't have a credit rating in the US, I wore a suit to look respectable, had a bank-guaranteed check, and waited in long lines to get a rental. This was unsuccessful. Eventually, I found an agent who would rent me a furnished one-bedroom apartment in Nob Hill, and I could use my Canadian credit card. This was good because I had brought few things with me, mainly nutrition journals and books. Friends who visited remarked on how old-fashioned the apartment was, and how unlike my style, but I didn't care because it was a bargain. The nicest thing about it was that there was a library on the ground floor, and I was able to use it as my office.

Once again, I started my process of writing to doctors and trying to convince them to let me see their patients. I was giving talks all over San Francisco, many unpaid because I was new and just needed to get out there. The unpaid talks were usually badly organized and few people turned up, but I didn't care, because sometimes there was a client. I learned that the more you get paid, the better you are treated.

Every time I gave a talk, I would print the program and use it for marketing. I would mail it to all the dietetic associations and corporations to let them know that I was available, but very few were impressed.

My practice was taking too long to pick up. Money was running out. After three months, I was in tears because I wasn't able to pay my rent.

I called my boys. Kimbal said it was the first time he ever heard me break down and cry.

They said, "We can pay your rent."

I wasn't happy about that. They insisted, saying that they had no time to spend their salaries anyway because they were always at work.

I began to look for a cheaper place that I would be able to afford. The only thing I could find was on the border of the Tenderloin, which was a rough neighborhood. Dirty, dark, smelly hallways, but affordable. My kids came along with my nephews to help me move. A friend with a truck picked up a bed a colleague had sold to me. We moved my few items to the studio apartment. Fortunately, I didn't have much.

Another dietitian gave me her practice at three fitness centers, as she lived ninety minutes away and didn't find it worth her while to drive that distance to see a few clients. This supported me just enough to stay in San Francisco a while longer.

On my fiftieth birthday, the year before, my children had given me a tiny wooden house and wooden car and said one day they would buy me both. I thought that was cute. Once my sons sold Zip2, they told me it was time to find the house and car I would like to buy.

Tosca and I looked in San Francisco, but she wanted me to move to LA, as she was living there. We went looking at houses in LA, too. At that time, I was booked for a talk on nutrition entrepreneurship in New York. When I arrived, I was blown away. In New York, the people walk fast, talk fast, think fast, and do what they say. I thought, "These are my people."

I said to my kids, "I'm moving to New York."

The kids said, "How can you just do that?"

I said, "I need some excitement."

In New York, I stayed on the couch of a client's business partner and went looking at rentals because I didn't know New York at all.

They said, "You have to live on the Upper East Side."

I said, "Can't I go downtown?"

They said, "No, nobody lives below Forty-Second Street."

Once again, no one would rent to me, as I didn't have a credit record. I offered to pay in cash, up front, for a year.

They said, "Only drug lords and prostitutes do that."

Someone recommended that I stay in a furnished apartment that would accept my Canadian credit card on a monthly basis. Eventually I found a tenth-floor prewar apartment on Twenty-Second Street between Park and Broadway that I could buy. It had large windows with a view of about thirty water towers. I was told that was really cool.

I thought I would be in New York for the rest of my life, because when you're there, it's the center of the world. Then I had a co-op problem, like everybody else, and I became disenchanted, as I was very sad.

When my daughter's twins were born, I went to LA to help her. She wouldn't let me return to New York, so I sold my apartment, gave away my plants and everything from my kitchen, put some items in storage, and sent some furniture to family. I stayed with Tosca for eight months, then bought an apartment. That was a great move, as I'm happy to be near two of my kids and seven of my grandkids in LA, although I still travel a lot.

It's always hard to move, even if you do learn each time. With every move, I would plan ahead, give away anything that wasn't worth moving, sell bigger items, put things in storage. That is quite a process. Then the first few years are always a struggle. It's lonely and you feel lost a lot of the time, physically and mentally. As I ran my own business, I had to let all my clients know of my change of address, even when I moved in the same city, but for me, it was worth it. I wouldn't recommend it to anyone unless they really think there is an improvement. If you think you can improve your situation, it's worth trying.

You need to have a reason to move. You may want to explore better opportunities, get away from bad situations, or just take a chance. It could be the best thing you do.

TWENTY

OUT OF CHARACTER

Push your boundaries

❖

O ften in life, you will be asked to do things that aren't very comfortable. For instance, public speaking. This is an area that terrifies many and is fairly common. You may have to get up and do introductions for a meeting, pitch to a client, or convince a bunch of investors that what you are trying to do is really worthwhile.

I've always been confident when giving talks; that's not a problem. In the nutrition world, I am very comfortable with my nutrition knowledge as I continue to study, taking seventy-five one-hour exams every five years to retain my accreditation and reading up on new research work every day.

In the modeling world, as a commercial model—which means I model for catalogs, airlines, hotels, teeth, hair, makeup—I'm very comfortable.

.   .   .

Now for the uncomfortable situations:

As someone new in a city, it's always uncomfortable to walk into a roomful of strangers. I've already addressed that.

Then there's the uncomfortable situations that have happened in my modeling career since I turned sixty: posing nude twice! When I was asked to model naked for *Time* magazine, I said, "No. I don't do naked."

They continued to pressure me to do the shoot. I called Kimbal and Tosca to tell them about the opportunity.

Tosca said, "You don't do naked."

Kimbal said, "Mom, it's *Time* magazine. It's going to be just fine."

He was right. It ended up being just fine.

When you are asked to do something outside of your comfort zone, it is okay to say no. I said no to nude shoots for fifty years. But I figured, *Time* magazine is a safe place to try it once. The photographer was well-known and did beautiful work, so that's why it was worth it.

I wasn't sure how comfortable I would be with the preparation, but they had me in a room with two women who helped me get ready with natural nails, hair, and makeup. Totally fine.

They sat me on the floor with a mirror in front of me, so I could see exactly what the photo would look like.

Then the photographer came in, a male photographer, and he took the photos and left. So that was fine, too.

They were tastefully done and were beautiful photos. In the

end, they moved the photo to the cover of the Health segment inside instead of as the cover of *Time*. My agent was not happy, and she said the photographer wasn't either, because that wasn't what they booked us for.

I wasn't very upset about not having my naked photo on all the newsstands. So that was fine for me!

New York magazine called my New Jersey agent, and they also wanted me to do a nude shoot. This time, they said they wanted to do the Demi Moore pose. This time, I would appear to be pregnant.

I was with Tosca, and I said, "You can't believe this—they want me to do the Demi Moore pose."

This time, she said, "Do it!"

I said, "Why would I do it?"

She said, "It's iconic!"

I didn't want to do it, but she changed my mind.

They wanted a natural look, with harsh lighting, because they wanted me to look seventy. I was only sixty-two at the time, and they wanted me to look much older than I was, and I didn't mind. I had often done that.

I wore nude underwear and pasties, but I still felt pretty naked.

They brought a pregnant woman to the shoot; she was having her baby that week. She'd forgotten she had a tattoo under her belly, so they had to photoshop that out. We were both photographed, and then they photoshopped her belly onto me, for the pregnant effect.

The picture was shown across the world, on TV shows and

in newspapers, with the cover line "Is She Just Too Old for This? New Parents over 50—Child Rearing's Final Frontier."

Funny enough, months after that, I was on a photoshoot, and people were happy I'd lost my baby weight. I told them I wasn't pregnant and I'm sixty-two!

Afterward, everybody said, "Did it make you feel free to do nude shoots?"

No! It was highly uncomfortable, and I felt quite awkward about it. If I didn't show it, it was because I'm a model and I'm a professional. If I did it, it's because I trusted both magazines. Now that I know what it feels like, it's not necessary for me to try it again.

There are many times when stepping outside my comfort zone has been a great opportunity. When I had to dance as Martha Graham for a photo shoot, that was way out of my league. I watched a video, as I am not a great dancer. I just copied the videos. Some of the shots were with the lead dancer of a ballet company. He said I should just fall into his arms. I did, and it felt wonderful. He was so strong. The photos were fantastic. I looked like a professional dancer. The problem is that since then, everyone wants me to dance in photo shoots!

When I did CoverGirl, they wanted me to dance on a rooftop, in heels. I said to them that I couldn't dance, but they didn't believe me because of the Martha Graham story. I had to convince them to bring me a choreographer. They did. She danced behind the camera, and I just copied her. Since then, many of my shoots have me dancing. Who knew?

When I did an editorial for Hypebeast, wearing hip-hop

street styles to appeal to another demographic, the millennials, I showed that grandmothers could model streetwear brands and look stylish. I actually had to try to remember how the stars on the TV series *Empire* danced. I wish I had paid more attention; however, people loved the shoot. That ended up being quite fun and opened up a whole new fashion arena for me. Because of that shoot, we got to show that fashion has no age limit.

What I have learned is that sometimes you could be uncomfortable with your style, but give it a try, and don't let anything like age limit you.

TWENTY-ONE

INSTA-FAMOUS

You're never too old to learn a new technology

◆

I'm grateful for technology. It's a frustrating and annoying process, but it's really been wonderful for me. Technology has been wonderful to my whole family. We never shied away from change that could improve our work, our lives, and the planet, and that included technology.

Technology has changed so much since I was a child. When I was eight, I helped my dad at his office, typing on a heavy, loud typewriter with a ribbon that I had to change by hand. Typewriters got better until finally, at the end of my thirties, I got a word processor. It was quite amazing. You could make corrections on it, but it couldn't save. You would print out pages, then retype them. It was the original "cut and paste"— you cut, you put pieces of paper all over the floor, and then you pasted them in a certain order. And then you retyped it. I retyped my first thesis fourteen times—my first master's degree took four years. My second one took only fifteen months. That was because by then, I had a computer.

There was still no internet, until around when I moved to San Francisco.

At that time, my sons were right on the cutting edge of technology. When my sons were launching Zip2, they often asked me to be the beta tester for their upgrades. If I couldn't follow along, they would make adjustments so that everybody would be able to use it. Once I printed out door-to-door directions early on, when they were building the internet company. After trying it out, I couldn't return from a trip, as I couldn't reverse the directions with all the one-way streets. We needed return directions—they added that in.

To promote my nutrition business, I made a deal with them: in exchange for giving a talk on nutrition to their employees, they would build my website. It was four pages.

I think I was the first dietitian to have a website. It was so useful for marketing, a welcome change from printed materials. When I was relying on brochures, they would quickly become out of date as information changed. Now I could just refer people to my website, and everything they saw would be fully current. I marketed my nutrition business from the late nineties through my website. Because of the website, I've been booked for many talks, media work, and spokesperson work. Around 2010, I started a website with my modeling portfolios showing five decades of work.

Social media has been a huge help to me in all my work. I have used Twitter mainly for sharing nutrition research and other news of interest; this forum has brought me interviews and speaking engagements about health, which I love to do. It's also very useful for getting feedback. When I post research work on Twitter, followers are quick to let me know what they like and don't like, what they need or don't need. It also helps me go in the direction where people are interested. I think it's great.

With Instagram, after posting editorials of a white-haired woman looking different, I took a chance with Julia and went to Paris at my expense. The intention was to invest in myself, which we all should do from time to time. We created street-style looks at sixty-seven during Paris Fashion Week. Although I wasn't invited to the top runway shows at the time, I made every moment an Instagram moment, dressing in different looks in the streets of Paris. I dressed in up-and-coming de-signer outfits and worked with a street-style photographer from France who we met via Instagram.

This investment paid off. It opened the doors for top run-way shows, CoverGirl, and more. Even now, years later, I'll go to modeling jobs where those photos are the inspiration for shoots. But overall, even if it didn't work out, I had a great time shooting for content, dressing up, and laughing with new and old friends. Because of social media, I was signed to IMG Models, became the oldest CoverGirl, and no longer have to go to castings for modeling jobs.

Social media connected me with the world of high fashion. A designer saw my Facebook photos and sent me an invite to his movie premiere in LA. I took a friend of mine; we didn't know anyone there. After I posted a photo of the premiere online, the designer asked me to walk in his runway show. I'd never walked in New York Fashion Week before. At sixty-seven, I walked my first couture show. I wore a beautiful white-and-silver gown and looked like a bride, although I had white hair. My friends in the audience said the guests screamed and clapped when I walked. They were so surprised and happy to see someone my age. For the finale, the designer asked me and one other model to walk with him on either side. That felt very special.

Once I saw the power of Facebook and Instagram, I announced on social media that I was going to New York. Many photographers reached out and asked if I would do a test shoot with them. I said yes to all of them. You never know which photos would turn out well, but it's worth it to try. This led to some terrible photos, and some really cool photos to post, and more requests for modeling.

Many people like to say that technology separates people or makes us lonely. But I haven't found that to be the case. It connects me with new friends, old friends, and potential clients. I also get last-minute invites to friends who see me in their city and connect right away. It's really incredible that we can speak to family and friends across the world, even see their faces. This is crazy and magnificent. I can FaceTime my twin every night. My grandchildren in California seem to have fun playing games with their New York or Colorado cousins, which is a great way for them to stay connected. When I think of all the miscommunications when we used to have to send a telegram, make a phone call, or write letters that would arrive six weeks later, modern technology is great!

. . .

It is true that technology can be hard. And every new technology is painful. With every update you're thrown into confusion. You make mistakes. When Instagram upgraded something, suddenly I had three videos of what I thought I hadn't posted, and I had to take them all down in the middle of the night. It can drive you crazy. You have to work yourself through it by finding the solutions on the internet. It takes a long time, and it's frustrating. But that doesn't mean I am too old for this. Maybe I'll follow my mom's example, as she started computer art at ninety-four, because her hands were shaking too much for fine art work. It's not age-related. Funny enough, when I had dietetic interns from NYU, Columbia University, and other universities doing their electives with me, they found me very advanced in technology, more than them. Tech can open up so many opportunities for you—for business, your health, or just for fun to connect. You're never too old to learn new technology.

TWENTY-TWO

ALL THE SINGLE LADIES

*You can be happy in love, and you
can be happy on your own*

✦

I give a lot of advice, but I don't give dating advice. I have been very successful in my life, except when falling in love. I've dated a lot, and I've liked some men quite a bit, but I haven't met anyone I wanted to live with for the rest of my life. Sometimes I say that my dating advice is: don't take advice from me! But my love advice is that you can be happy in love, or you can be happy on your own. If you cannot find the right person for you, find love with family, friends, and work.

If you think marriage is the key to happiness, talk to your friends who are married. When I was young, no one told me that you can't be happy on your own, although everyone in the sixties was getting married at twenty. No one was alone. I'd be curious to know how many of those couples are happy or still married. It is wonderful to have a good life partner, like my parents', my brothers', and my twin's marriages. They found happiness. I haven't been married since I was thirty-one; that's forty years ago. People have said to me, "You will find love when you least expect it." I least expected it most of my life, but I've never found love. I've tried but did not find a man who made my life better than I can myself.

I started dating at thirteen because of my twin sister, Kaye. She met her boyfriend at the dancing school we worked at when we were thirteen, and since she was not allowed to go out alone with him, we had to double-date. He told her it was easy to get a date for me. But I rarely met a young man who was interesting enough to go out with. When I did date, a man would be crazy about me, then want his distance, then was crazy about me, then want his distance; I never understood that. I called these push-me, pull-me relationships. It was hurtful.

Once I started modeling at fifteen, the boys thought I was too popular to be asked out on a Saturday night. My twin sister and her boyfriend would take me to the drive-in theater. They were always fine with that. Saturday nights were an important dating night for me, and I was always sad when I didn't go out. When I got married, I compromised for an abusive man who cheated on me. I tried to do everything that my husband wanted me to do, and I was miserable. When I got out of that marriage, my whole life improved, even though I had to struggle in other ways. After my divorce, I really didn't have a clue how to date. If a man asked me out, I would go out. If he was annoying or uninteresting, I would not go out anymore. If I liked a man, he would end up dumping me or cheating on me, mainly cheating on me. Then if I looked at his track record, he cheated on his wife and his girlfriend, too. He was not going to change for me. The man I was engaged to in my early thirties also cheated on me.

I also had three kids, so anyone I dated had to like them. Most men weren't interested in my kids and would prefer not to have them around. Then there were the guys who needed me to make compromises in order for the relationship to work—and I would! One had a clothing company, and he only wanted me to wear his cotton knit clothes. He didn't want me to wear anything else, so I would wear those clothes. Then there was the man who said that I was too sophisticated, and so I started wearing jeans and T-shirts for him.

All the guys would want me to change, but I never asked them to change for me. I finally realized that if I was going to have a relationship at all, I didn't want to have to compromise. And I didn't. My relationships still didn't improve. Over the years, I was fooled less and less. If there's any consolation, I did learn. I had been a jerk magnet in my teens and in my twenties, and I was somehow still a jerk magnet in my thirties. In my forties, I dated some wonderful men, but none that I wanted to spend the rest of my life with.

I decided to try internet dating in my early fifties, when I was in New York. I figured I would try thirty dates, and if I didn't fall in love, I was not going to continue. It was easy to get those dates because I put a modeling photo up on the site. Some of my dates were my age, some twenty years older, some twenty years younger. None of them looked like their photos.

I learned quickly that lunch or dinner dates meant three hours of listening to a man complain or just talking about himself the whole time. Or they just complained about their ex-wives. Neither topic was very interesting to me. They didn't even know I had kids, because they didn't ask. They didn't ask anything about me.

The kind of man I wanted was one who, after I'd had a long day's work, or traveled for a talk or modeling job, would be happy to see me. Was that too much to ask? It seemed that it was.

Around that same time, Elon had a dachshund and Yorkie, and two dogs had a puppy.

He said, "I'm giving you the puppy."

I said to Tosca in horror, "I'm living in New York. For the first time I'm alone. There's no responsibilities except for myself. Nobody even knows I have kids. It's just wonderful. And now Elon wants to dump a puppy on me." And Tosca said, "It will stop you dating jerks." And you know what? It stopped me dating.

When I would go out with a guy, he would be arrogant and irritating. I couldn't cope with these lengthy complaining sessions, so I started meeting them for just coffee. After thirty minutes, I would say, "I need to go walk my dog." It was a great excuse.

When I would go home, my dog loved me to bits. It did stop me dating, in the nicest of ways, because there was no point.

If you want to fall in love, you must date. You need to get out and meet friends who have friends who could possibly date you, or try online dating (but meet in a public coffee shop and don't share your information until you've met a few times for coffee). Dating is hard. Relationships are complicated. But that shouldn't deter you. My dog makes me happier than any relationship I've had, but I'm seventy-one, so don't go that route yet. You can still try. But you have to do what makes you happy. If you're with someone you don't love but you enjoy their company, like a best friend, you might be fine with that. If that person makes you happier when you are with them than when you're alone, then that's fine. But if you are unhappy with someone, it's best to get out. There is no point in being with someone you don't enjoy.

The world makes such a fuss about romantic relationships, but what about friendships? I have friends I met when I was eleven. I was in my forties when I met Julia. I have new friends I met just this year.

When I met Julia, we were both struggling and trying to figure out how to make it work. Yet we were never competitive; we just wanted each other to succeed. That's part of why we became lifelong friends.

One of the elements of a successful friendship is how long it lasts. Another is how enriching it is. If you have friends who detract from you, who tell you that you aren't good enough, that isn't a friend you want to keep or whose advice you want to get.

Julia will say that we've always been each other's greatest cheerleaders, and I agree. We also enjoy each other's company and have a similar sense of humor. We're punctual, and we like to work hard. We are always in touch. When we are together, we do a lot of traveling—Milan, Paris, Doha, Budapest . . . When we are apart, we FaceTime. It's a comfort to feel at home with your friends and be able to be yourself completely.

Up until I was twenty-one, I lived with my parents and siblings, and then with my children. Now, I love to live by myself. Between my friends and work, I have many invites to dinners or parties. Our family is often getting together for launches: it may

be a restaurant, a new car, a nonprofit, a film, or a rocket. Or my grandchildren come and sleep over and build forts out of the bedsheets and the pillows.

My life is very full with friends and family, without a romantic relationship, but I also enjoy a quiet night in with my dog, Del Rey. Even if it is a Saturday night.

My mom used to say, "If

you are unhappier when he is with you than when you are alone, get out of the relationship. If you are happier when he's with you than when he's not with you, then you stay in the relationship."

I'm glad to report that Del Rey and I are in a very good relationship.

PART FIVE

———— ◆ ————

Health

TWENTY-THREE

EATING WELL MAKES YOU HAPPY

Plan your meals

❖

I was being interviewed by a young woman who kept commenting on my vitality. "You're so energized! You have so much energy!" She is right.

I need to have a lot of energy to go to meetings, walk in runway shows, and fly around the world for speaking engagements, shows, and modeling. I need energy to walk my dog. I need it to pick up my grandchildren from school and look after them for hours or days. Energy keeps my mind sharp and my mood up.

When I was obese, over 200 pounds, and would give talks or counsel clients about healthy eating, I would say that genetics had taken over, as everyone in my family was overweight. I would make it sound like a joke and tell people to eat well and don't eat like I do. This didn't give me confidence, because I had lost control. I loved eating a lot. Fried chicken, fries, burgers, ice cream, chocolate—anything and as much as I liked. Afterward, I would go into a food coma because I was so tired from eating so much. The physiology here is that all your energy goes to digesting food, and you have little energy for the rest of your body. When you are eating well, you have a lot more energy. That was always the surprise that my clients had. When they changed their eating habits, they discovered energy they never knew they had.

The important thing is to focus on having hope and being excited about the day. What you really want is to age in good health. Most of the main reasons for poor health in later years, like diabetes, Alzheimer's, and heart disease, are related to nutrition. Eating healthily is the best way to age well. It can also affect your mobility. You may not worry about it now, but look at your family and the struggles they are going through. You can decrease your risk for many health problems.

The best diets to follow to keep your body and mind healthy include the DASH diet, Mediterranean diet, and the Flexitarian diet. All these diets require planning ahead.

Your plan should always start with writing down everything about your diet as it is. When I used to see clients, I would find out every detail of their daily eating routine. What time they woke up, what they ate for meals and snacks. What time they ate and what they would choose. And what time their activity was. This would give me a good idea of what they think they are eating. The next question would be about alcohol:

how often, what type, how much. The recommendation is one drink per day for women and two drinks per day for men. The research does show these amounts have health benefits; however, if you don't drink, you don't have to start drinking now. Some clients would lose a lot of weight when they followed my alcohol recommendations, which means they were drinking more than they remembered. Sometimes they would say they had hangovers and told me how terrible it was. I often wondered why they would want to do that twice. As I am not a big drinker, I can't understand this problem. With alcohol, you also lose your willpower. I do. After my favorite drink, rum and Diet Coke, I'm happy to nibble on any foods. There are certainly no salads nearby, so it's usually chips, fries, and nuts, and I can eat a lot of them. There go my food goals. If you find alcohol makes you lose your willpower, that's an obvious reason to decrease your alcohol habits.

I would ask my clients if they drink coffee or tea, how many cups, with milk (and recently a plant beverage), with sugar or sweetener. I would recommend a maximum of three cups of coffee, three cups of tea, as well as a maximum of three diet sodas per day. In my case, on a normal day I'll drink two cups of coffee, one cup of tea, and one diet soda.

People are always horrified when I order coffee with milk and a sweetener. According to fad diets, all should be avoided. That's absolute nonsense. Follow science and common sense, and enjoy your coffee again. I love black tea with milk and a sweetener. Although green tea is said to be so much better for you, with more antioxidants, I don't like the flavor. You don't have to drink nutritious beverages if you don't like them. Some teas are for weight loss or nighttime. But you should be wary of these. If they seem to work, there are other substances causing this weight loss or sleepiness.

There are many reasons other than hunger that cause people to overeat. I would ask clients if they would eat more when they were feeing anxious, stressed, tired, bored, depressed, lonely, and/or happy or when they were socializing. Some would say they eat for all those reasons, some for some of those reasons. The only good reason to eat is if you are hungry—so I would work with clients on all the other reasons. Without changing these causes, you can't change how you eat.

If you overeat when you are anxious: What is the cause of your anxiety? Is it something that can be resolved? Are you scared of something that may or may not happen? Sometimes we are scared of things that never happen to us. Of course, at other times, horrible things happen to us that we weren't expecting and we're not anxious about them.

If you eat under stress because of your work, you need to decide if you want to change this, too. If you love your work but you don't like your colleagues, how do you change that? Can you talk to them? Move to a different division of your company? Or do you actually have to find another job? You need to be happy at work. It's easier to eat well when you're happy. Otherwise you go for comfort foods, like the cookies or muffins in the office kitchen. Your other option is to eat as well as you can, avoid all the temptation around you, and keep healthy food at your desk and in the kitchen's fridge.

If you eat because of a personal relationship, with a loved

one who threatens to leave you if you don't lose weight, you have to make a decision. Just so you know, that is not always the real problem. It certainly wasn't with me. I dropped to my skinniest to make my boyfriend happy, and he still cheated on me and complained. So, extra weight was not the problem. He just used it as an excuse. You need to eat well to make yourself feel good, not others.

If you overeat or eat poorly when you are tired, then you have to have the right foods around you at all times. When I was a mother with three babies, there was no rest, and I rarely slept through the night. At that time, I kept only healthy food around, so that I couldn't be tempted. Even now I keep only healthy food around me.

When you are eating because you are depressed, you need to find out why you are depressed and address it. Once my clients dealt with their depression and began to make an effort to eat better, they felt more confident and positive. They started fitting into their clothes that were too tight and shared their happy stories with me. The same with people who ate when they were lonely or bored.

Some of my clients were happy eaters. Happy eaters love to eat, especially high-fat, high-salt, high-sugar foods. The more food on the table, the better. There was a study to show that if you present an obese person with one plate of pasta, they will happily eat most of it, but if you present them with four plates of different pastas, they will be even happier and eat much more. I understand this well, because with only one pasta, we will have flavor fatigue. We also like to finish everything on our plate, and if there are four plates, we probably can't finish them all, but we will certainly try. We are very happy when we over-eat like this but very sad the next morning. You have to work hard at self-control even when happy. Similarly, if you love to socialize and would drink a couple of glasses of wine or beer, and then eat whatever snacks were available, which are definitely not salads, it is easy to overeat on crackers, cheese, chips, peanuts, fries, and mini-burgers. Everyone else is drinking and eating—how come they don't gain weight? That's because some people are naturally lean—or maybe they don't snack as much as you. If I am invited out for drinks, I usually order a rum and Diet Coke, or a fruity martini, and look for something healthy, hopefully some kind of vegetable or shrimp appetizer that isn't fried. I also don't go out for dinner afterward. That snack is my dinner. It is so high in calories that I am actually full and I'm not hungry for dinner. This takes training, willpower, vigilance, persistence. But I always feel better at the end of the night. Remember how good you feel after eating well when socializing, and keep reminding yourself.

A good eating plan starts first thing in the morning. I may have oatmeal or a bowl of high-fiber cereal with 1 percent milk and a few slices of banana. It needs to be simple and quick. If you aren't creative with food, when you find something that works, you can eat the same thing every day.

Later in the morning, I know I'll be hungry, so I plan ahead and am ready to eat fruit and yogurt, or whole wheat bread and peanut butter. That's followed by lunch and another snack, because late afternoon is a common time to be hungry. Recognize it as a real hunger and not anything due to boredom, fatigue, or stress. Don't go six hours without food or you'll get too hungry! If you are the type of person who has trouble making the right afternoon choices, don't let it get that far. Plan to eat a filling snack before you're starved, at about 3:30 p.m., and you'll be ready to enjoy your meal at suppertime.

I like an early dinner, and I like to eat light at night. Whenever I can, I will fast between 7:00 p.m. and 7:00 a.m. If I am starved, I can't go to bed, so then I will have a glass of milk or a half cup of cottage cheese. You'll notice that I'm really eating every few hours throughout the day so I don't get too hungry, as well as choosing small portions, so I don't feel too full. If I get too hungry, I risk ruining my mood or feeling depleted. That's how I know it's time for my next meal or snack: I feel a little bit hungry.

Eating more often, choosing healthy foods in smaller portions, and waiting until you are hungry are all part of the foundation of a good eating plan.

I'm not an accomplished cook—I leave that to Kimbal. On holidays, Elon and I stay out of his way while he creates a feast in the kitchen, with Tosca's help. But at home, I still need to feed myself, even though I don't particularly enjoy cooking. I will often make a large soup out of all my leftover vegetables from the week, along with rice and beans (dried beans that I've soaked overnight). I'll freeze the soup in single portions so I can readily defrost, heat, and eat as needed.

At my seventieth birthday, my kids gave a speech at which they joked about the way I fed them when they were growing up. High-fiber cereals with milk, plenty of fruits, vegetables, peanut butter sandwiches, and bean soup. I still eat that way, because healthy food does not need to be complicated.

It also does not need to be expensive. We grew up frugal, as my parents had been through the Great Depression. There were no expensive meals and no waste. I've eaten on a budget all my life. I still eat on a budget, although now I don't have to. The problem is, people with a low income think they need immune-boosting, or detox, or energizing juices, which are expensive. They also think they need supplements because of all the ads. People always say we should eat organic. But so many people cannot afford organic and can't really find it. Don't let that stop you from eating your fruits and vegetables; just wash them well.

Here are some ideas for planning ahead: Pack a peanut butter sandwich and a banana, and order a café latte. Or an egg sandwich, or a cheese and tomato sandwich, both of which you can put in the refrigerator at work. You can boil four eggs and eat them over four days. Eat an apple instead of a cookie to make you feel great afterward. Eating a yogurt is not complicated. Drinking a glass of milk when you're rushing is not complicated. Everything is nearby, if you make the effort. The first time you make a mistake, by not eating breakfast then diving into a donut at 10:00 a.m., it's not your fault. The second time you do it, it *is* your fault. You need to plan for this. If you don't eat breakfast, it's probably because the night before you ate too much for dinner and you weren't hungry. If it's because you're too rushed, wake up five minutes earlier. I can eat cereal while I'm checking my emails. You can, too.

. . .

For me, I have no choice. I either plan to eat healthily, or I gain weight because the options available are not healthy. I know that if I am eating high carbs, I will be hungry in two hours. If I have eggs on my toast, I will be hungry in four hours. Fat and protein keep you fuller longer, as they take longer to digest. But I love high carbs, so at home I definitely eat every two hours. When I travel, I will order oatmeal in my room for breakfast. Portions are always large. So I eat half at 8:00 a.m., and half at 10:00 a.m., and then go to lunch at 12:30 p.m. not starved. When you are starved, you cannot think. And high-fat foods are very tempting and frequently nearby, like croissants and chips in the office cafeteria.

I often say I have to plan ahead or it's a slippery slope; it becomes harder to turn it around. I have to turn it around right away and eat healthily, otherwise the weight just piles on. If I overeat at dinner, I gain three pounds and my pants are tight. It takes me three days to lose it. This happens less and less every year.

This is the way I live when I am at home, and I take these principles with me when I am on the road. Nowadays, I travel a lot for work. Whether I'll be away for three hours, eight days, or weeks, I know I must keep my eating to plan. If I can't plan my meals every day because I won't be home, I think ahead about what my schedule is going to be like and what foods might be available. If I'm not sure, I bring a banana, because a banana can keep me going for an hour or two.

I've learned that if I need a plan at home in order to eat well—and I do—that is even more true when I'm traveling. Last year, I had a few events to attend that were scattered around the world. Over the course of six weeks, I flew from LA to New York to London to New York to Milan to London and then back to LA. In every city, I had modeling jobs, people to meet, places to see, and a well-planned schedule. That takes a lot of energy.

First, I always keep snacks, such as nuts and dried fruit, in my bag for emergencies. If you're starved, you'll put any food into your mouth as quickly as possible, and good choices are never nearby. I just need a small snack to take away the ravenous feeling and help me make a good food choice for my next meal.

Second, when I'm staying at hotels, I call ahead to have them take all the snacks out of the room. I don't need all those tempting chocolates. I also ask them to empty the fridge, as I'll need space for my own food. I'll go to the local market and get milk, cereal, fruit, nuts, and yogurt. I might even buy a whole wheat roll with some butter, cheese, and tomato if I think I would need a more substantial snack.

Third, I'll make my own coffee in the morning and use the milk I've purchased, which is better than the half-and-half they leave in the rooms. I don't want to go out starved. I would rather just have a yogurt or a glass of milk beforehand, so that I can make the best choices. I would love pancakes, but I know the wheels would come off if I ate them, as I won't stop until I finish the plate. Learn from your mistakes and plan ahead.

If I'm heading out for dinner, a snack before I leave prevents me from finishing the breadbasket before I've ordered my meal. At meals, I'll often enjoy a vegetable soup and whole wheat bread instead of a main course. I never rush myself, and everything is planned in my head.

Many followers ask me to tell them what
exactly I eat every day. This is an average day's
food intake, when I'm at home:

Breakfast

I fill a large container with my favorite high-fiber breakfast cereals, such as Cheerios, Bran Flakes, or All-Bran Buds, plus dried cranberries or raisins, walnuts, or sunflower seeds, enough for two weeks. I shake it up and eat about one cup with half of a sliced banana and 1 cup of 1 percent milk.

Coffee with 1 percent milk and one packet of artificial sweetener

Snack

Half a cup of yogurt

1 apple

1 cup of black tea with 1 percent milk and 1 packet of artificial sweetener

Lunch

1 cup of homemade bean and vegetable soup

One hour later

2 slices of whole wheat bread, 2 teaspoons of butter, 1 tablespoon of peanut butter, and lettuce

1 diet soda

One hour later

1 orange

Snack

Café latte with 1 percent milk and 1 packet of artificial
sweetener
1 tablespoon of nuts

Dinner—6 p.m.

Salad consisting of 1 cup of lettuce, 1 slice of onion, half a
tomato, 1/4 cup of garbanzo beans, 1 boiled egg, 2 ounces
of canned salmon, 1 tablespoon of sunflower seeds,
2 tablespoons of vinaigrette

Snack

1 cup of 1 percent milk or 1/2 cup of low-fat cottage cheese
12 grapes

SOUP RECIPE:

1 package of 15 Bean Soup, soaked overnight, boiled for
90 minutes. The last 20 minutes I add wild rice and any
vegetables and seasonings that I have.

TWENTY-FOUR

ENJOY YOUR FOOD AGAIN

There is no magic pill

❖

People talk a lot these days about superfoods. Meanwhile, they're terrified of bread. They're scared of milk. They're concerned about being short on protein. Everybody wants protein powder, protein supplements, high-protein bars. Why, I don't know. As a dietitian in private practice for forty-five years, no one's ever been short on protein. But nobody wants to hear common sense. They want a magic pill instead.

I am often glad I stopped counseling five years ago, now that modeling and speaking engagements have taken over, because fad diets have overtaken any voice of reason. I am now paid to tell audiences to follow science and common sense. It's about time.

It's true that fad diets do lead to rapid weight loss, because they are removing your favorite foods, processed foods, high-fat foods, alcohol. People have tried to eat healthfully, and failed, many times. It is hard to avoid temptation. They find it easier to exclude a food group completely. For example, excluding carbs altogether will mean that they won't eat pizza, chips, fries, hamburger buns, pasta, and desserts. This they find easier than eating well because they don't understand that eating well means limiting those high-calorie foods, too. When I tell them that over my counseling career, no one gained weight on whole wheat bread, they agree that makes sense. But they don't eat whole wheat bread. They would rather have a bagel and croissant. These people don't eat high-fiber foods, so that's all they need to change. Choose high-fiber cereals, bread, brown rice, beans, nuts, fruits, and vegetables. I know most people don't eat any beans, and very few eat enough fruits and vegetables. You would think it's common sense, and it is. When a diet says you should have bacon as a snack instead of fruit, somewhere in your mind you must say: that's not a good idea. But instead you say: yum, I can eat bacon.

If you follow a healthy diet and replace your favorite foods with high-fiber, nutritious foods while also avoiding processed foods, high-fat foods, and alcohol, you can enjoy your food without going to extremes. And as a bonus, you'll also avoid being an absolute pain at a party or dinner.

The gluten-free diet has taken off; again, everyone is losing their common sense. They think a gluten-free cookie is better than a piece of fruit or a slice of whole wheat bread. Very clever marketing. Funny enough, when I ask people if they enjoy barley soup, they say yes. I say it contains gluten. They say they're not allergic to *that* gluten. The look on my face in response to this does not usually endear me to anyone. Gluten is also present in rye, but that doesn't seem to be a problem either.

In processed foods, gluten is replaced by other ingredients that may not agree with you, so if you're having stomach problems, that could be the cause. Also, gluten-free products are not as delicious.

If gluten-free means you don't eat a whole pizza every night and you lose weight and feel fabulous, why don't you try replacing a whole pizza with a whole wheat sandwich? You don't have to go to extremes and annoy everyone. Most people don't know where you find gluten and what it is. "I'm going gluten-free and high-protein," someone will say. I tell them gluten is a protein. They don't know that. And they don't appreciate my information.

People want hope. Fad diets give you hope and sometimes give you rapid weight loss due to extreme restrictions and lower calorie intake, so they will always be popular.

I remember, as a nutrition student, being interviewed on the radio about nutrition. My professors and everyone at the dietetic department spoke Afrikaans and couldn't speak English, so they sent me. I felt that I wasn't qualified because I hadn't graduated, but I studied the periodic tables for the essential nutrients and the Krebs cycle for metabolism, so I was on top of my game. What I found out was the type of question I received was, are potatoes fattening? I soon realized that people just want to know the basics, not physiology and biochemistry.

Researchers don't understand why the public believes these

fad diets. Thirty-five years ago, when an eighty-year-old, prestigious nutrition researcher at the University of the Witwatersrand in Johannesburg was asked to give lectures, I needed to drive him and his wife to their conferences. The reason they needed me was that after his brilliant talk about nutrition and the latest research, the questions included "What do you think about the Atkins diet?" He didn't know what that was. I could answer that question and let him know that there was a bestselling book out that promoted high animal fats and low carbs. This confused him, because research did not show that to be a healthy diet. Yes, fad diets have been around a long time. But they do not change your lifestyle. People have a hard time sticking to them. The gluten-free diet does lead to continued weight loss if you keep on following it, because it does stop you from eating pizzas and cookies. You should eat food you enjoy and choose an inexpensive and delicious balanced diet. Fad diets require just as much planning as healthy, nutritious eating.

I was having lunch in London with two very intelligent, successful women who were talking about their fabulous nutritionists.

They said, "She draws our blood every month."

I said, "Why is she drawing your blood?"

"Oh, because our hormones are all out of whack."

And I said, "So then you have to buy pills from them?"

"Yes, yes, you have to buy all their pills."

"And how many thousands of dollars a month does it cost you?"

"Oh, five thousand dollars for the test, and then a few thousand a month."

I said, "You can stop all of that."

"Oh, no. I'd gain weight. She really saved me."

And I said, "But were you eating poorly before you met her? What did you change in your diet?"

"I ate a lot of cheese, so I took the cheese out and I lost weight."

I said, "You didn't need anything else, except taking the cheese out."

They didn't appreciate my reasoning and didn't listen to me. They still are true to their nutritionists, who have no qualifications.

Some people are also spending a lot of money on juices, $40 per bottle. That is ridiculous. If you really like juicing, make it yourself so that you get all the fiber that goes with your vegetables and fruit. You can get extra nutrients from fortified cereals, fortified beverages that have been thoroughly researched to show that they contain the ingredients stated on the label, in the right amount.

I say there is no complicated secret to healthy eating; just follow science and common sense. Every time you think you can or cannot eat a food, go on the internet to reliable sources like universities or articles written by dietitians. Don't look for articles by doctors who have zero to little training in nutrition but have a bestseller, a holistic nutritionist (whatever that is), fitness trainers, or people trying to sell you juices, powders, or pills. Dietitians just want to sell you good health and are much less expensive. They will give you confidence to eat well and control your eating habits. People don't understand the difference between registered dietitian-nutritionists (RDN) or registered dietitians (RD), and nutritionists. The former two are experts in nutrition who have graduated from a university and interned at a hospital. They can separate fact from fiction, plan meals, and help you translate the science of nutrition into healthy food choices. They understand the importance of diet in the prevention and treatment of many disease conditions such as diabetes, cancer, hypertension, and heart disease, and their advice can enhance your quality of life.

Then there are the nutritionists, who do not need any qualifications, who may hold beliefs that are not based on research. They are usually more expensive and sell products. Don't be fooled! Before you write a check, look at their accreditation. A giveaway is the letters RD or RDN after their name. But even if they have an MD, consider what they are trying to sell you before you agree to a program. Anyone peddling fear of eating normal foods or promising cures and miracles from supplements, powders, or products that have not been shown to have any benefits is not out to help you but to pad their own wallets. They're the cure for your insecurity, not your health issues.

Forget the trends. You don't need to eat kale to be healthy! You can, but you don't have to. I'm a supertaster, which means that I find certain foods too bitter to eat, including kale. I don't like it, so I don't eat it. I eat other vegetables, the ones that I like.

There will always be those people who are disappointed that you don't eat kale. Tell them that kale is not the secret to health. The "secret" to health is eating more fruits and vegetables and whole grains and legumes and dairy, and eating what you enjoy, in small portions, when you are hungry.

The best health plan is the sustainable one—the one you will stick to, even when you are stressed, or tired, or too busy to pay a lot of attention to it.

You don't need a pill. You need a plan.

TWENTY-FIVE

CHOCOLATES GO HOME
WITH THE GUESTS

Keep temptation out of reach

◆

The route to poor food choices is confusion and temptation. When it comes to temptation, if you don't plan ahead, usually the food closest to you is high in fat or sugar, such as chips and chocolate. Once we start eating those foods, we cannot stop. These are our trigger foods. We cannot resist them, and we can't stop eating them. We can eat them even when we are full. For me, there's always room for fries or chocolates, even if I feel stuffed.

When I had my nutrition practices, with every client, the first goal I gave to each one was to plan to have healthy snacks nearby, like a yogurt and a piece of fruit, or a slice of bread and peanut butter. I would often say, "Eat three apples before you eat a cookie." They never managed to eat a cookie, because after one apple, they were full. So that's a good strategy. Sometimes I will overeat on vegetables and fruit and gain a little weight, but nothing like I would gain if I'd binged on junk foods.

After a huge and delicious dinner to celebrate a birthday, the waiters brought out the desserts for the table, I didn't hesitate to indulge.

I happened to be sitting next to a six-foot-four guy. After a while he said, "You eat more than me."

I told him I don't eat that way all the time, but this was worth it. Those desserts were delicious! Every fiber of my mouth was happy. I gained three pounds. The next day, I went back to my regular, healthy style of eating, and it took a week to lose those three pounds. In my twenties, I could lose that weight in two days. In my seventies, it takes a week. Sometimes it's worth it.

If you're going to indulge, do it because it tastes wonderful, not because you've been triggered by a sad or stressed feeling. I've learned over time not to waste my calories on desserts that aren't delicious.

It's helpful to become fussy. I was at a meeting where there was a large assortment of cookies. I didn't want to resist them, so I chose the most decadent-looking one, with chocolate and nuts. After one bite, I found it had no flavor. It was very disappointing and just wasn't worth eating, so I put it back on my plate and didn't touch it again.

If you taste something and it's not delicious, leave it.

When people bring me chocolates and treats, they smile so nicely. But I am horrified. I tell them that they cannot bring me this kind of food because I will finish it all. They say to just eat one piece every day, but that is not in my genes. They have to take the treats home, or I will give them away. Or even throw them away, if I have no one to give them to. It is just not worth the stress of knowing that this magnet in my kitchen is attracting me all the time. I cannot keep any sweet treats in my home, because they are trigger foods. What does that mean? It means I can't just taste a small piece of chocolate; it sets off a trigger reaction. It makes my taste buds tingle, and I want to polish off the whole chocolate box. For many people it would be something savory, like chips. For other people, it's ice cream. The important thing is to know which foods are your trigger foods. If you have a trigger food, whatever it is, keep it out of the house and out of reach.

Avoiding your trigger foods is about weight loss, but it is also about disappointment and feeling unhappy. It affects your mood. We don't want to be unhappy.

If you do stress eat or overeat, don't waste more time feeling stressed about eating. A better strategy is to skip the guilt. Ask yourself, "Did I enjoy it?" If the answer is yes, don't berate yourself. Carry on as if nothing happened. At your next meal, eat fruits and vegetables, lean protein, whole grains, and beans. The next day, resume your healthy routine. Meals don't have to be perfect. And neither do you. One unhealthy meal does not make or break a healthy lifestyle. If you eat healthily 80 percent of the time, you will feel fantastic all of the time.

If the answer is no, make a note to remind yourself next time that unhealthy snacking didn't even help, so why bother?

Focus on remembering the good feelings that come with

sensible and healthy food choices. If you eat healthy foods, in the right amounts, you will feel energized and nourished.

When I'm at home, it's so much easier to plan good eating. Never spend your own money on foods that will sabotage your healthy habits. If you have kids, buy a treat that the kids like, not one you like. If I wanted to give my grandchildren treats, I let them choose small ice creams or a single cookie. That way, there wouldn't be a box for us to finish.

Know your weaknesses, keep them out of reach, and you'll feel better every day.

TWENTY-SIX

KEEP MOVING

Choose activities that you enjoy

◆

When I'm at home, I walk every day. Actually, I go for four short walks, because my dog wants me to take him out. I reap the benefits, too. I love the feeling of a nice walk, and so does Del Rey.

I encourage some type of activity every day. But I don't believe in pushing so hard that it hurts. Physical fitness doesn't need to cause pain. I've learned this over time.

I've never been good at sports. When I was young, I was the nerd, and Kaye was the athletic one. She was great at sports and so are her kids. I'm not, and neither are my kids!

You just need to plan for daily activity. If my clients were not active at all, I would find out what they are willing to do. Do they like to walk, run, play tennis, go to the gym? It needed to be something they enjoyed. If they were extremely obese, I would just ask them to walk slowly for thirty minutes per day; I didn't want to stress their heart, knees, or back, until they had lost twenty to fifty pounds.

If they didn't have time for any activity, I would ask them to walk in place and do stretches while watching television. That is what I did when my children were young. I only started going to a gym in my mid-forties, when the children had left home and I could afford the gym fees. I'm sure my kids were embarrassed when their friends came over and I was doing jumping jacks in front of them, but I didn't care.

Being active alone doesn't lead to weight loss, but it does motivate you to feel good, which helps with weight loss. It is also essential to move the body for good health. Even while I'm writing this book, I am taking time to stretch on my yoga mat in my living room, walk my dog, and exercise for forty minutes per day—thirty minutes on the stationary bike and ten minutes with light weights.

When I was writing my first book, I was working out a lot, doing step and yoga classes at night. I overdid it and started getting pains in my buttocks. So naturally I started working out even more. This pain went into my thigh, then down my right leg. It was so painful that I could not touch my knees. If I dropped something on the floor, I would leave it there for a few days until I could cope with the pain of getting on my hands and knees to pick up everything I had dropped. To get into the bath took half an hour. Only someone who has had this extreme burning sensation down one leg knows how painful it is. You look healthy, but you cannot sit down or stand up.

I went to six chiropractors; they didn't want to adjust me because I had a double herniated disc. I went to massage therapists; they were scared to touch me, too. I could walk without pain, but any other movement caused fire down my leg. It's weird to look healthy and complain about the pain.

I called my brother, who is a neurologist, and he sent me to a neurosurgeon.

In Canada, fortunately, surgeons don't get paid more if they do surgery, so they're not going to operate unless they think it's essential.

The surgeon said that he didn't want to do surgery until my foot went numb. That would mean my nerves were dying. I said I didn't care, I just wanted to stop the pain. Now I'm glad he was conservative, because it healed in eight months. I've had many friends who've had back surgery, and it may have been better if they had lived through the pain.

I still had to work! When I would do runway shows, they had to have two dressers for me. One to put my clothes on from underneath, and one to put them on from on top. Sometimes I'd do eight shows a day. I would just lie on the floor with my feet on a chair between shows. It was hard for them to believe how much pain I was in, because I looked just fine when I was standing still.

I was consulting for a firm and wanted to go to a research meeting in Philadelphia because I love hearing what scientists have to say. It was so painful to fly, but I wasn't going to miss out just because of that. I brought my lumbar roll with me and used it every time I sat down.

When I got to the meeting, I had to lie on the floor.

Afterward, we were all going out to dinner.

"Fortunately," said one of the scientists, "we won't have to get a chair for Maye. She'll be on the floor."

I thought I would never be well again. I used to watch people jogging or working out and think, "I'll never be able to do that again." I would envy people who could actually move around and sit down without pain. All I wanted was pain-free mobility.

After about six months, I could feel I was getting better, as I could bend over and touch my knees again. By eight months, I could touch my feet, which meant that I could have a proper shower again.

What I have learned is you should listen to your body; don't push it past pain. You don't always need an aggressive training schedule. You don't always need bigger weights. You don't always need to push harder. You just need to move, because over-exercising can cause injuries.

So can grandchildren.

I was running after my grandkids recently, up the stairs. I turned a corner and twisted my knee. After that, I was hobbling and in excruciating pain. I didn't know what had happened, so of course, I went to Dr. Internet, and I saw that you can have knee injuries if you are elderly or if you are an elite athlete.

Well, serves me right for being an elite athlete.

Kimbal's friends, who are all elite athletes who have had

numerous knee surgeries, told me I would probably need a knee operation. They said it was only six weeks for recovery. I said I didn't have that kind of time. I had to walk in New York Fashion Week two weeks later!

I iced my knee and kept it elevated, just like Dr. Internet suggested.

At the fitting, they said, "There are going to be lots of stairs."

I was freaking out because I could walk, but stairs were painful.

The show was at the Met Opera, and there were four flights up and four flights down. I had to walk them four times. They gave me flat shoes, which was great. I certainly wasn't going to complain, because I'm a professional. I just coped with the pain. But it hurt.

I got through that show, and when I came home, I called my doctor, who told me to put Bengay on my knee and see an orthopedic surgeon. Good news: it was a sprain and would heal over time. I didn't need surgery.

I've managed to succeed through a lot of hard times because I've been in good health, and so have my kids. I am so grateful for that. All it takes is a little bug, or a minor mishap, and you're down for days. That's when you realize that health is everything.

Nowadays, I don't push myself too hard. I will work out on the stationary bike, and if my knees hurt, I go on the treadmill. If that hurts, I do stretches and weights. A day or two later, I can get on the stationary bike without pain. I'm more cautious when I run after my grandchildren. When my knee hurts, I wear a knee guard.

Just like the elite athletes.

TWENTY-SEVEN

MIX WITH HAPPY PEOPLE

Healthy relationships are good for you

◆

My clients would say I was cheaper than their psychologist because when they ate better, they felt happier, stronger, and more confident. Emotions do play a large role in your health. If you are unhappy, it's harder to have the strength and energy to eat well. You're looking for comfort foods, and they are always high in fat.

Mixing with friends and family who make you happy is very good for your health. As a scientist, this is not something I have studied, however it is common sense. If you are in a good relationship, you feel physically healthy. If you aren't, you feel beaten down and sad.

I'm fortunate to have a happy family and a happy extended family. We love spending time together and laugh out loud until we cry. Taking care of family is a value my mother instilled in me by example. She always took care of us, making sure we were well-fed and encouraged to explore different interests. And she made sure we took good care of our own kids. When I was getting divorced, my mother said to me, "Family first." What she meant was that I had to put my children ahead of everything else. I stayed married for the sake of my children. I then got divorced for the sake of my children.

"Family first" is how my family operates. It is important to us to get together regularly. That isn't always easy for a group of forty very busy people who live in various cities, but we make it a priority.

One year, our whole extended family went to Costa Rica together. Another year, we chose Costa Brava, in Spain. We look for a place where we can book a small hotel and fill it with family.

Part of the reason we have such a nice time together is because there is room for everyone to do what they want. Some will do a sport while some will be reading. Others will swim or go for walks. Some will be sleeping; some will be eating. On these trips, you know that you have people there who love you, but you're also allowed to do your own thing. We're not clingy. If activities are organized, you can join in—or sit out. If you want to spend the time on your phone, that's okay. If you want to be on your laptop, that's okay, too.

At sunset, Kaye goes for a swim on her own. She can swim for three hours a day; she's a great swimmer. She doesn't care if anybody's with her or not. I will sometimes follow her, but she swims much faster than I do. And after thirty minutes, I'm tired, but she just keeps on going. She just glides through the water.

Sometimes we'll go and visit the nearby towns. Whoever wants to go, does. Or we'll arrange dinner at a restaurant and try to fit forty in.

One evening, all forty of us turned up for dinner. All the grandkids were running around and screaming, and there was so much noise.

I said to Kaye, "I can't bear the noise anymore."

She said, "Me, too!"

We took sandwiches and walked down to the beach. We sat alone and watched the sea and had a peaceful evening together.

Sometimes it's just me and my kids and their kids. The Thanksgiving just after Tosca's twins were born, we were planning to spend the holiday at Elon's home.

SpaceX was launching a rocket, and Elon wanted us all there, so I got an email the night before saying, "Flights are booked tomorrow morning to fly to Orlando."

I called Tosca to tell her, but she was already asleep. I managed to get hold of the nanny, and I said, "You've got to go to Tosca's condo, and wake her at six a.m., because at seven a.m., she has to get to the airport for the flight."

You can imagine how frantic we were with all these last-minute travel plans. We had the two little babies with us, who were howling. For those hours, we were trying to comfort them and looking apologetically at all the passengers around us.

When we got to Orlando, we all took a bus to the launch at Cape Canaveral. We had takeout turkey dinner with everybody in the NASA building.

I enjoy having a close family, as we can trust each other at all times and look to each other for support. We have been through many hard times, but we've stuck together. That is really special. Sometimes people tell me that their families are nasty. I don't believe it until I meet them and I see how they continuously throw insults at each other. I think about my ex-in-laws. It was a screaming match at every meal. I don't know how you change that other than not spending time with your family. If you have a family that makes you unhappy, find friends who make you happy and make you smile. If your family can't be there for you, friends can certainly support you in the good times and the bad times.

When we take care of each other, everyone benefits.

TWENTY-EIGHT

IT'S GREAT TO BE SEVENTY-ONE

Keep smiling

❖

Some of my friends are my age. Many are younger than me. All of them are excited for life. My hashtag on social media is #ItsGreatToBe71 because I'm enjoying it so much.

People seem to be scared of aging, based on the comments I read on social media. When they see my posts, it makes them feel better about their future and their wrinkles. I also get many interviews about why I am enjoying my age and why older people should be revered, appreciated, relevant, and stylish.

One reason I'm not afraid of aging is that every decade of my life has been better than the last. My twenties were terrible except for my three wonderful children; my thirties were pretty bad, too; my forties were so busy just to survive; in my fifties I was new in New York and trying to get my business started and finding friends; and in my sixties, I was more settled with my kids and grandkids and work. Now, I'm busier than ever. I didn't expect that, but I'm loving it.

The other reason I am not afraid of aging is that my mother set quite an example. When my father passed away, my mother was sixty-one. He was seventy-three and died in a plane accident, along with my twin sister's husband. It was utterly tragic—it seemed impossible. In our minds, he was Superman.

They had been so happily married, we thought she would never recover. We didn't know what would happen to her; she had always been there with him, helping him, supporting him. We were so wrong. She blossomed. In her mid-sixties, she started taking art lessons. She took up wood carving, pottery, and painting. She traveled around the country, doing landscapes and houses, in oils and watercolors. She would exhibit her work regularly in Pretoria.

She was also a photographer and began exhibiting her photos and winning awards. You will notice that some of her photos of us in the desert are beautiful. We didn't appreciate how much talent she had. She passed her silver hair on to me but not her artistic talent. In her seventies, she then took up etching, a difficult process by which you use a needle to etch a metal plate, then use various chemicals and machinery to eventually press it onto paper. She got all her own equipment and learned how to use it all. She was in South Africa's *Who's Who Book of Artists*. She worked day and night on her art. All this led to a twenty-two-year career as an artist in South Africa.

When she was eighty-six, she moved back to Canada and started all over. It was when Zip2 was sold, and we had the resources to fly my mom and sister to set them up in Canada and be nearer to the family. Other people were worried that my mom would miss her friends. When I called and asked her about it, she said she wasn't worried at all, as all her friends were dead. She was drawing, still doing etching (she had brought her equipment with her), and exhibiting regularly. At the time, my sister Lynne was living with her and teaching dancing and took up digital art at fifty-nine, too. But my mom was just getting started.

At ninety-four, she was shaking too much for fine art, but instead of slowing down, she took advantage of technology and learned how to make digital art. At ninety-six, she was shaking too much for even that, so she retired and then read voraciously and followed all our travels on a map. She said in her nineties she was the happiest she had ever been. I think we have something to look forward to.

I remember going with her to the "oldies" tea, a social gathering of seniors, in a small town in Alberta. It was a miserable experience because they were all complaining.

We left, and I asked, "Are they becoming grumpy as they get older?"

She said, "No, they were grumpy when they were younger."

So, if you are a grumpy person, you can practice now to change; otherwise you're going to be grumpy when you get older.

My mother was incredible to be around. Her wits were about her until she was ninety-eight, when her body gave in and she died. Kaye was with her and said that she was laughing that morning. My mom never had a fear of aging. She never even spoke about it. She always looked fabulous—she wore bright red lipstick everywhere and always liked to wear earrings when she went out. In her older years, she had beautiful, long white hair. She was always nicely put-together (except for the paint on her clothes).

She was always positive, and so was my father. I remember him as a person who always looked for joy. Even the back of his business cards read "Keep Smiling." He brought that feeling into everything he did. They never raised their voices, and I never heard them arguing.

If you get to be alive long enough, problems repeat themselves. When you hear about something terrible or somebody is horrible to you, you can just say, take a number. You've had that happen to you before, it upset you terribly, then the next time less terribly, and now you can brush it off.

We have had deaths in our family, because we have a huge family, and that will happen. The first time it happens, it is devastating. You don't think you can recover, but then you do. You can even talk about people who have died in your family and not fall apart. That's the good part about aging.

When I would visit my older sister, who had colon cancer, I would take my dog. Then my dog got old and became ill. I was very upset. She said, "You should live longer than your dog," so I should realize that. I think about this reality check, even now after my sister has passed away. She kept her sense of humor until the end. At some stage I took her to the supermarket. She had to hold onto the cart because she was so weak. We ran into somebody she knew, who told her she looked great, she had lost weight, and asked her what diet she was on. She said, "Cancer!" and then laughed.

For my seventieth birthday, I had two parties. One in New York was organized by CoverGirl and *Harper's Bazaar*. It was full of people in the fashion industry, models and friends from the time I lived there. In LA, Elon, Kimbal, and Tosca organized a huge party. It was a beautiful day. There was a slide show with my photos through the ages, balloons outside the house, special cocktails, and an ice-cream bar, professional dancers, and a DJ with a saxophone player. I was surrounded by so many of my friends and family. A school friend I had met when I was eleven years old in my hometown was there. Elon, straight from the Tesla gigafactory in a T-shirt. Julia, my best friend, with her husband. The dietitians I had worked with over the years had created a binder of stories from colleagues, a collection of appreciation and gratitude that moved me to tears.

If you learn anything from me, let it be this: don't be afraid of aging, and mix with friends who are not afraid of aging. Have fun with your friends, of all ages, who like you because you are fascinating, interesting, intelligent, confident, and maybe stylish (in your mind). Listen to others, be good to others, no matter their ages. If someone tells you you're too old, especially if you are dating that person, say goodbye.

Aging is great. We are wiser as we get older. We are more confident—that was a nice surprise I have experienced. And we also know we have to get rid of jerks in our life quicker. I guess you could say I look forward to the future with enthusiasm.

At this stage of my life, I'm having the best time ever. First of all, I wrote this book so other women can have a better life. That makes me feel good, and hopefully you, too.

I've just started in my seventies, and I can't wait for what's next.

MAKE YOUR PLAN

Start now

W hen I began writing this book, I took a trip to New York City. I had lunch with my book editor and attended a CoverGirl launch event, and I recorded a podcast with the editor in chief of *Allure* magazine. Julia was there, too, choosing clothes for me.

I was staying at a very beautiful hotel. I had just gotten off the phone with Tosca, who was on set doing a movie. I was texting Kimbal, who was opening a restaurant that week, and I was sitting in the lobby, watching Elon's SpaceX launch on my iPad with pride—and I had a memory of being in that hotel before. I was in my early fifties and living in New York City. My dietetics practice was just starting.

I remembered coming to New York to do a fashion shoot, right there in that hotel. Nothing in the hotel looked any different, although I suppose I looked different. My situation was different.

After the shoot, everybody went to have a drink in the bar at the restaurant. I wanted to join them, but I didn't stay, because I couldn't afford to pay for my own drink. Perhaps someone would have paid for me. But what if they hadn't? So I left. If you can't afford it, you don't do it. I didn't feel deprived or sorry for myself. I never said, "One day I'll be back!" I certainly didn't imagine that if I ever did come back, this is what it would look like.

I just kept working hard, making a new plan, and moving forward.

Maybe that's why I wake up each day feeling optimistic. I've lived with plenty and I've lived with nothing, and I've seen that you never know what will come next. I am in good health, enjoy my work, love my family, and have great friends.

. . .

In health, in business, in life, there is no quick fix. All you have is hard work, optimism, and honesty; common sense and a plan.

You can make a plan, but it doesn't always work out. So then you have to make another plan. Your life will be full of ups and downs, like a roller coaster. The ups will be great; the downs will be hell. And when you're down, you need to plan how to climb out. As you age, the downs are less tragic, less painful, and less hurtful, because you've been through them before.

You have to decide for yourself when you want to be happy. When is that? Why delay changing your career, improving your health, having a happy family and friends, loving your life? At times, I never thought I would be happy. Ever! And then I made a plan to get out because continued unhappiness is not a way to live. So make your plan now.

Acknowledgments

Thank you to my late mom, who set a wonderful example as an intelligent, hard-working, gentle, wise, and confident woman. I'm sure she would be happy about this book, as she read my first book aloud, line by line, twenty-four years ago.

Thank you to Kanessa Tixe, who nagged me for two years to write a book. I didn't think I had an important enough message until we started traveling worldwide and sharing my story with the media, new contacts, and audiences at talks.

I'd like to thank my literary agents, Paige Sisley and Sally Harding, who were so excited to work with me. They enjoyed and were inspired by the advice of my former book, and felt I had a larger story to tell.

I'd like to thank my stylist and best friend, Julia Perry, for making me look fabulous and always wanting what's best for me. Thank you Ali Grace Marquart, for checking all my contracts, including this one, and always legally protecting me.

I'd like to thank Sandra Bark, who took my stories and sorted them into chapters.

I'd like to thank my editor, Emily Wunderlich, for spending many weeks making the chapters compelling and keeping me focused on my messages.

I'd like to thank Viking Penguin Random House, for being as excited about this project as I am.